S ck
innovation

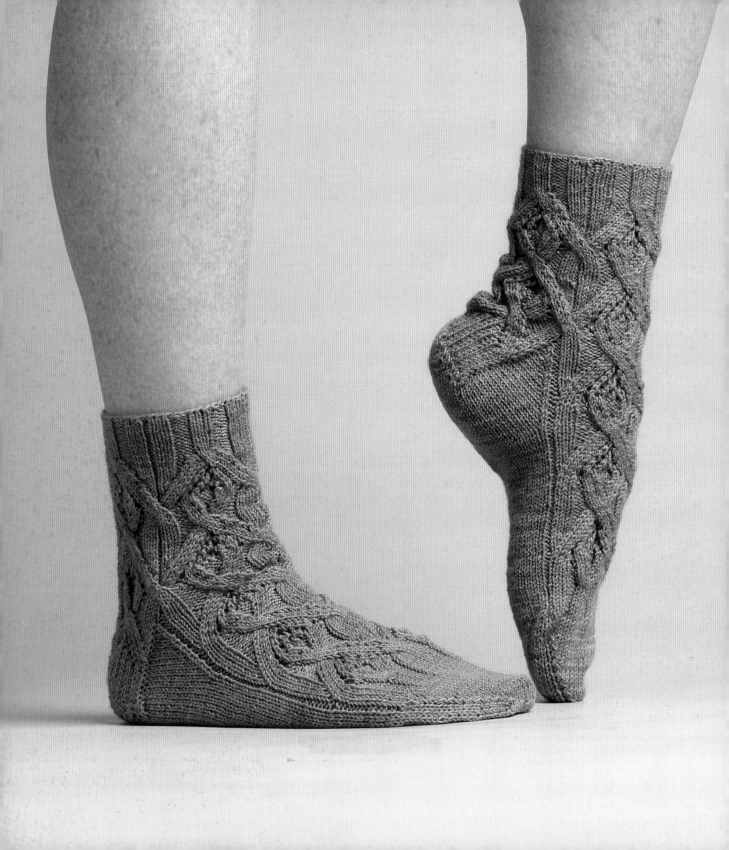

Sock innovation

KNITTING TECHNIQUES
& PATTERNS FOR
ONE-OF-A-KIND SOCKS

cookie a

INTERWEAVE
interweavestore.com

Photography, Joe Coca
Photo styling, Ann Swanson
Art direction and design, Connie Poole
Layout, Pam Uhlenkamp
Production, Katherine Jackson
Technical Editor, Kristen TenDyke
Editor, Anne Merrow

Interweave Press LLC
201 East Fourth Street
Loveland, CO 80537-5655 USA
interweavestore.com

Printed in China by Asia Pacific Offset.

Library of Congress Cataloging-in-Publication Data

Cookie A.
  Sock innovation : knitting techniques & patterns for one-of-a-kind
socks / Cookie A., author.
      p. cm.
  Includes index.
  ISBN 978-1-59668-109-5
  1. Knitting--Patterns. 2. Socks. I. Title.
  TT825.C657 2009
  746.43'2041--dc22
                        2008043191

10 9 8 7 6 5 4

acknowledgments

I would like to thank my parents, without whom I would not have existed; my husband, who has been extremely supportive of my knitting obsession; and Kristi, who is responsible for the knitting monster within me. The socks in this book are named after people who have helped shape my life. Without them, I would be a different person and possibly sock-less.

A heartfelt thank you goes to the sample knitters for their beautiful knitting: Jeannie Cartmel • Erin Cowling • Jessica Dekker Alyson Johnson • Lisa Lowery • Celia McCuaig • Monica Nappe Kristie Naranjo • Jenny Noland • Angela Palisoc • Isela Phelps Stacey Rothchild • Emily Spence • Tan Summers Linda Stahl • Chelsea Welp • H. E. Wintermute

And of course, I <3 BobaKnit.

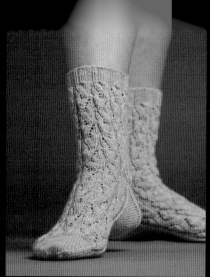

contents

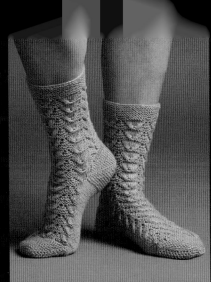

Patterns 56

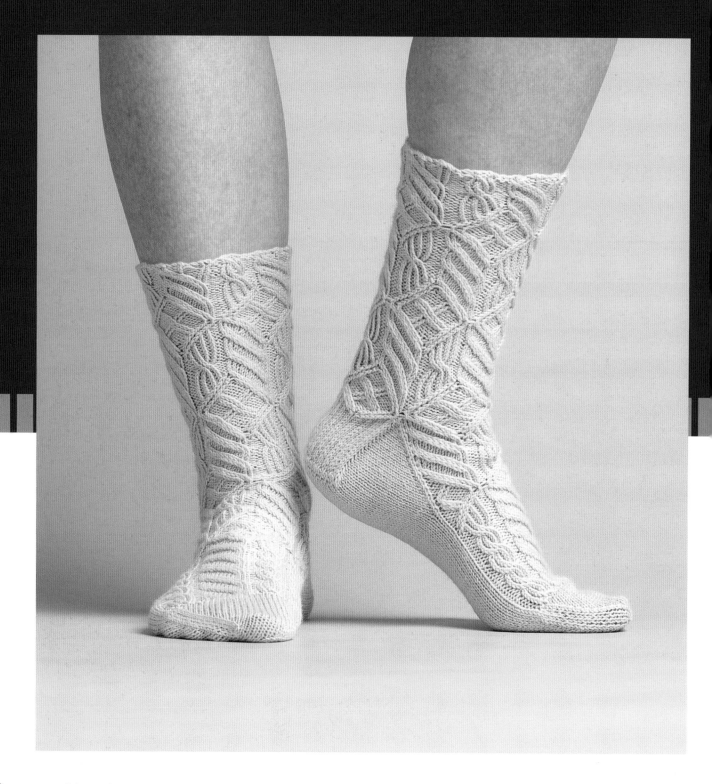

design and socks

I am often asked where my inspiration for patterns comes from, and I have a difficult time answering. My favorite subject in school was mathematics, particularly theorems and proofs—the more abstract the better. I enjoyed the fact that grand theorems could arise from a few simple definitions and rules. A similar principle applies to knitting, where there are a limited number of manipulations that can be performed. Everything boils down to three actions: wrap yarn around needle, stick needle through loop, and pull yarn through loop. Depending on the order or the direction of these three maneuvers, infinite possibilities exist.

My love for socks began when I moved to California. The weather was too warm for my wool sweaters, and Kristi (my BKFF—best knitting friend forever) raved about socks so much I thought I would try them. I was hooked.

Socks are a perfect first step toward learning to design, as a wide variety of skills and considerations must be taken into account. Any technique that can be used in a sweater can be done on a smaller scale in a sock. They provide the perfect learning ground for knitting design.

When I think about sock design, I generally start with an abstract idea, a line I want to follow, or a texture. My inspiration doesn't come directly from mathematics; I'm unlikely to knit a Fibonacci pattern, use cellular automata, or think of ways to incorporate crazy topological spaces. But my entire approach to life involves abstract thought rooted in mathematics. An elegant proof is one that is simple, involves a bit of insight that isn't considered obvious, and proves something that is greater than the sum of its parts. An inelegant proof is one that is done by brute force or is overly complex. I find exactly the same to be true of knitting. Taking simple components and combining them in a way that is greater than the sum of its parts is the essence of good design. The alignment, placements, visual lines, textures chosen, and how they coordinate—these are all subtle nuances that differentiate a great sock from a good sock.

Stitch pattern idea

twisted stitch motif

alternating short vertical panels

← like parallel angled lines
- how many can fit?
- spacing?
- row gauge?

BIASES AND PREFERENCES

I have biases and preferences that will become apparent. All the socks in this book are knitted from the top down, and most have ribbed cuffs, a flap heel with gusset, and stockinette wedge toes. I find it easier to design from the top down for several reasons. The pivotal part of sock design begins with the division for the heel flap and instep. Depending on the patterning chosen for the leg, this division can be complicated. Beginning with the cuff gives a sense of how the stitch pattern is progressing before having to decide exactly how to divide. With a toe-up sock, these decisions must be made in advance, and there is less room for correction. I'm an impatient knitter, so I like to begin and make designs on-the-fly as I get a feel for the stitches on the needles.

Another advantage to top-down design is that the first few inches of the sock can be used as a gauge swatch and tried on different parts of the foot—the ankle, the heel, and the foot. With a toe-up sock, you can only try on as far as you have knit. Ankle fit is often the trickiest part of sock fit, and it is best to try on the fit there sooner rather than later. Nothing is worse than knitting 70% of a sock and then discovering that it won't go past your heel!

I am biased toward ribbed cuffs, flap heels, and stockinette wedge toes in pattern writing because it is easy to swap any of these components for a different type, but the most difficult ones to calculate are ribbed cuffs and flap heels. Substituting a picot hem cuff or plain hemmed cuff for a ribbed cuff is much easier than the opposite. My preference for the stockinette wedge toe is based purely on comfort and simplicity. I find more interesting places in the sock to assert fancy details, and my wide toes appreciate the breathing room.

HOW TO NAVIGATE THIS BOOK

Each chapter builds on skills and terminology from previous chapters, so it may make sense to read straight through. There are useful tables scattered through the book:

Inverse Stitches (see pages 25 and 27)

Mirrored Stitches (see page 40)

Heel Turn Numbers (see page 15)

The remaining chapters cover the major components of what I believe to be good design. While the information is targeted toward socks, many of the concepts can be applied to any garment. If you are not currently interested in designing socks from scratch, use the information for customizing existing patterns.

If you are impatient to begin a sock, skip directly to Sock Design (page 50) or to the patterns on page 56. Refer back to the earlier techniques as needed.

I hope this book will enable knitters to take more control of their knitting.

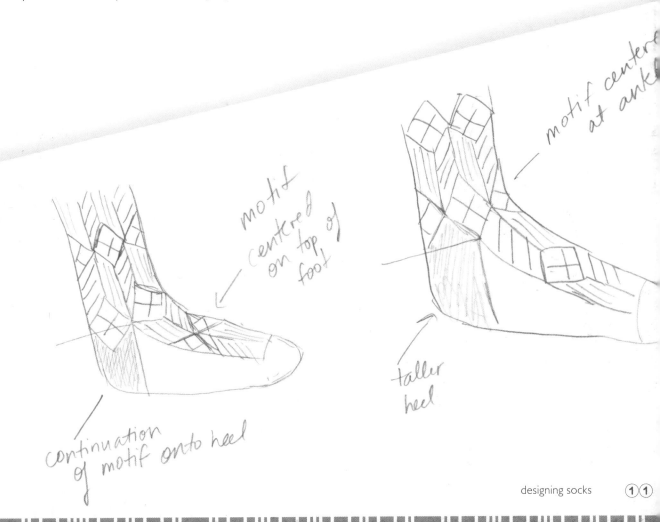

motif centered at ankle

motif centered on top of foot

taller heel

continuation of motif onto heel

sock techniques

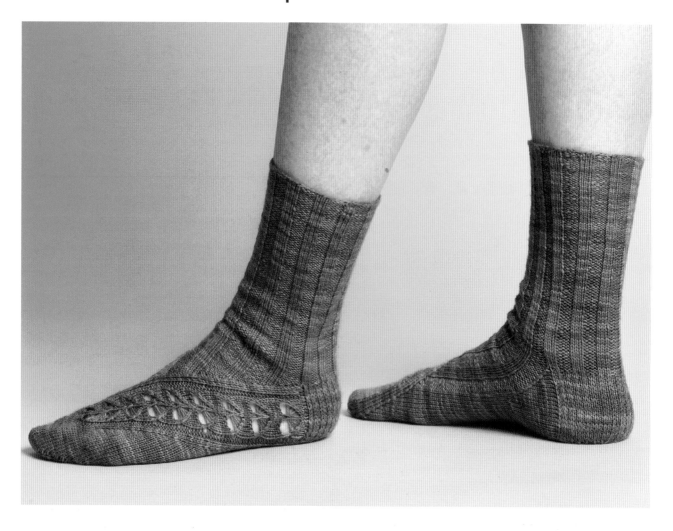

Aside from the main stitch pattern area of the sock, there are great opportunities for detail in the cuff, heel, and toe. In general, it is easy to interchange one type of cuff for another. The same is true for heels and toes. Some options to consider are described on pages 14–20, but feel free to experiment with other variations. Any edging or border can be used for a cuff. The toe doesn't have to be stockinette; it can be ribbed, moss stitch, or anything you'd like. The possibilities are endless.

Basic Sock Outline

The basic pattern for a sock knitted from cuff to toe can be adapted in any number of ways for a truly original sock.

Stitch markers are referenced throughout this book to mark the left and right sides of the sock and the beginning of the round. Depending on your circular knitting method—double-pointed needles, two circular needles, or one circular needle (magic loop)—you may be able to rearrange the stitches so that the marker placements for the left and right socks fall between the needles or at the division in the magic loop. Knitters using double-pointed needles can position the beginning of the round so that it falls between two needles, while knitters using circulars may need one stitch marker for the beginning of the round.

CUFF

Cast on the necessary number of stitches and join in the round, being careful not to twist. Work the cuff pattern (ribbing, picot, or any other edging or leg pattern) in the round.

LEG

Transition from the cuff to the main stitch pattern(s) for the leg. If the gauge for the cuff pattern is different from the gauge for the leg, increase or decrease as necessary. (See Transitioning from One Stitch Pattern to Another, page 48.)

Work the main stitch pattern in the round until the leg measures the desired length.

HEEL FLAP

Set aside about half the stitches for the top of the foot. The remainder of the stitches will be used for the heel. It is not necessary to divide at the beginning of the round; it can occur anywhere in the round. The heel placement should be determined by other elements in the sock, such as which components should remain on top and where the new beginning of the round should occur. Avoid placing the beginning of the round on top of the foot, or in the middle of the heel if the heel will be continued in pattern.

For a basic sock, work a standard heel flap and turn, ending ready to work a right-side row.

SHAPE GUSSETS

SET-UP RND: Slip 1 purlwise, knit halfway through the heel turn stitches and place a marker to indicate the center bottom of the foot as the beginning of the round, knit the rest of the heel turn stitches.

Pick up and knit 1 stitch in each slipped stitch along the edge of the heel flap plus 1 stitch between the base of the heel flap and the instep stitches. Place a marker to indicate the right side of the foot.

Work top of foot in rectangular pattern. Place a marker to indicate the left side of the foot. Pick up and knit 1 stitch between the instep stitches and the base of the heel flap and 1 stitch in each slipped stitch along the second edge of the heel flap.

Knit to beginning of round.

ROUND 1: (decrease round) Knit to 2 stitches before marker indicating right side of foot, k2tog, continue in the established pattern across top of foot, ssk, knit to marker indicating beginning of round—2 stitches decreased.

ROUND 2: (even round) Knit to marker indicating right side of foot, work top of foot in rectangular pattern, knit to marker indicating beginning of round.

Repeat Rounds 1 and 2 until desired foot circumference is reached.

Many sock patterns will keep the foot circumference and the leg circumference the same. If your feet are wider or narrower than the circumference of your foot or if you are using a textured pattern on the top of the foot, the stitch count for the foot and the leg may not be the same. Decrease the amount you need for your foot. Remember, you can try the sock on as you go along. If the sock is for someone else, I recommend cutting a piece of cardboard with the desired circumference (a rectangle with the width of half the circumference of the foot) and trying the sock over that until the right fit is achieved.

FOOT

Continue working even rounds (as from the gusset) until the sock measures two inches less than the desired length from the back of the heel. Measure the length of the sock while it is on a foot, since the row gauge can change when the sock is stretched.

TOE

Work a 2" (5 cm) Wedge Toe.

These ribbed cuff patterns flow into the leg patterns.

Cuff Options

The apparently simple ribbed cuff can be the most complex to design. Select a cuff pattern for form as well as function.

RIBBED CUFF

There are many different flavors of ribbed cuffs, from a basic 2x2 to a more complicated 3x3x3x3x3x1. Ribbed cuffs are great for flowing directly into a main pattern stitch as well as offering elasticity at the top of the sock.

HEMMED OR PICOT CUFF

Hemmed and picot cuffs are the same except that the turning row on a picot cuff has eyelets that result in a feminine picot edge. With a provisional cast-on, stitches can be picked up and worked together with live stitches, eliminating the need to seam the cast-on edge. Use smaller needles for the inner hem so that the hem will lie more smoothly. The directions that follow are for a 6-row cuff; this can easily be altered by working fewer or more rows before and after the turning row.

1. Using smaller needles, provisionally cast on (see Glossary) the desired number of stitches (must be an even number for a picot cuff).

2. Work 6 rows in stockinette stitch.

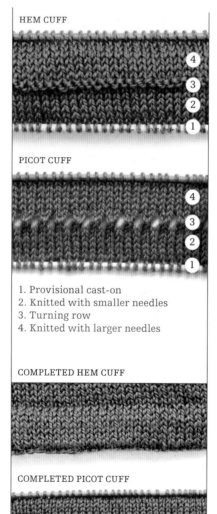

HEM CUFF

4
3
2
1

PICOT CUFF

4
3
2
1

1. Provisional cast-on
2. Knitted with smaller needles
3. Turning row
4. Knitted with larger needles

COMPLETED HEM CUFF

COMPLETED PICOT CUFF

3. For a hemmed cuff, create a turning round by purling one round. For a picot cuff, create a turning round by working [yo, k2tog] for 1 round.

4. Switch to larger needles and work 6 more rows in stockinette. Remove the provisional cast-on and place the revealed stitches on smaller needles.

Work the cast-on stitches together with the live stitches by knitting each live stitch together with 1 provisional stitch across the round.

PATTERNED CUFF

A cuff can be any pattern, even the same pattern as the rest of the sock. The possibilities for the cuff are unlimited. Any edging that can be used on other garments can certainly be used on a sock. The cuff below uses a combination of garter stitch and ribbing.

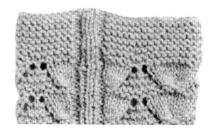

These three heels show different ways of transitioning from the leg pattern into the slipped-stitch heel.

Heel Options

The choice of heel is most important for comfort and ease of construction, but it is a particular concern when working with multicolored yarn.

FLAP HEEL AND TURN VARIATIONS

My favorite heel construction is the flap heel and turn. The flap part is a rectangle, which can be done in any pattern. Slipped-stitch heels are particularly popular because the slipped stitches offer reinforcement for the heel area—a common place for holes to develop. No matter what pattern is chosen for the heel, the first stitch of each row should always be slipped purlwise with the yarn held to the wrong side. This makes picking up stitches for the gusset easy. The longer the heel flap, the larger the gusset will be (see outlined areas below).

After completing the heel flap, I prefer to work a pointy trapezoid heel turn because I find the fit to be nice and tight around the back of the foot. General directions for turning a heel with a pointy trapezoid follow. **X**, **Y**, and **Z** refer to numbers in the table below right based on the number of stitches that are in the heel flap when ready to turn the heel. The heel turn is worked back and forth using short-rows.

End the heel flap ready to work a right-side row.

ROW 1: (RS) Sl 1, k**X**, ssk, k1, turn work.

ROW 2: Sl 1, p**Y**, p2tog, p1, turn.

ROW 3: Sl 1, knit to 1 st before gap created by turn on previous row, ssk to close gap (1 st from each side of gap), k1, turn.

ROW 4: Sl 1, purl to 1 st before gap created by turn on previous row, p2tog to close gap (1 st from each side of gap), p1, turn.

Rep Rows 3 and 4 until all stitches have been worked—**Z** sts rem.

HEEL STS.	X	Y	Z	HEEL STS.	X	Y	Z
19	11	6	13	41	21	4	23
20	12	7	14	42	22	5	24
21	11	4	13	43	23	6	25
22	12	5	14	44	24	7	26
23	13	6	15	45	23	4	25
24	14	7	16	46	24	5	26
25	13	4	15	47	25	6	27
26	14	5	16	48	26	7	28
27	15	6	17	49	25	4	27
28	16	7	18	50	26	5	28
29	15	4	17	51	27	6	29
30	16	5	18	52	28	7	30
31	17	6	19	53	27	4	29
32	18	7	20	54	28	5	30
33	17	4	19	55	29	6	31
34	18	5	20	56	30	7	32
35	19	6	21	57	29	4	31
36	20	7	22	58	30	5	32
37	19	4	21	59	31	6	33
38	20	5	22	60	32	7	34
39	21	6	23	61	31	4	33
40	22	7	24				

STOCKINETTE SHORT-ROW HEEL

Even though a flap heel and turn uses short-rows, it is not considered a true short-row heel because it doesn't require the use of wraps and turns. A short-row heel is similar to the flap heel and turn, but instead of a rectangle and trapezoid, it is constructed with two trapezoids. A short-row heel can be worked over any number of stitches, but when worked over the same number of stitches the short-row heel is tighter and smaller than the heel flap and turn.

Short-row heels are most often worked in stockinette. At the end of each row, the last stitch is wrapped and turned. During the first trapezoid, each row gets progressively narrower; on the second trapezoid, each row gets progressively wider, and the stitches that were wrapped from the previous rows must be picked up and worked.

SET-UP ROW 1: (RS) Note edges of heel flap (the back of the sock between the left and right sides), knit to 1 stitch before the left edge, wrap and turn (see Glossary).

SET-UP ROW 2: (WS) Purl to the last stitch, wrap and turn.

NARROW ROW 1: (RS) Knit to 1 stitch before first wrapped stitch, wrap (i.e., wrap the last unwrapped stitch in the row) and turn.

NARROW ROW 2: (WS) Purl to 1 stitch before first wrapped stitch, re-oriented wrap (i.e., wrap the last unwrapped stitch in the row) and turn.

Repeat Narrow Rows 1 and 2 until the number of stitches between the innermost wrapped stitches is about one-third of the original number, ending ready to work on the right side.

WIDEN ROW 1: (RS) Knit to first wrapped stitch, pick up wrap(s) (see Glossary), knit stitch together with wrap(s), wrap next stitch (that stitch is now wrapped twice), and turn.

WIDEN ROW 2: (WS) Purl to first wrapped stitch, pick up wrap(s) (see Glossary), purl stitch together with wrap(s), wrap (that stitch is now wrapped twice) and turn.

Repeat Widen Rows 1 and 2 until 1 wrapped stitch remains on each side, ready to work a right-side row.

NEXT ROW: (RS) Knit to first wrapped stitch, knit stitch together with wraps; do not wrap or turn work.

To close the gap at the edges of the heel, lift strand between needles from back to front using the left needle tip. K2tog.

Resume working in the round in pattern until 1 stitch before the last wrapped stitch. Slip this stitch knitwise to the right needle. Close the gap by lifting the strand between the needles with the right needle tip from back to front. Insert the left needle into the 2 stitches on the right needle and knit them together through the back loop, as if completing an ssk.

Knit the last wrapped stitch together with wraps.

Knit to the left edge of the heel and continue working in the round for the foot.

GARTER-STITCH SHORT-ROW HEEL

A garter-stitch short-row heel is similar to a stockinette short-row heel except it is worked back and forth by knitting every row. Wraps don't have to be picked up and worked because they will blend in with the garter stitch. However, after working back and forth for the heel there will be gaps formed at both sides of the heel from the turning. These gaps can be closed by picking up a stitch to the outside of the heel and knitting together to close the gap.

SET-UP ROW 1: (RS) Note edges of heel flap, knit to 1 stitch before the left edge, wrap and turn.

SET-UP ROW 2: (WS) Knit to the last stitch, wrap and turn.

NARROW ROW: Knit to 1 stitch before first wrapped stitch, wrap (i.e., wrap the last unwrapped stitch in the row) and turn.

Repeat Narrow Row on right and wrong side rows until that the number of stitches between the inner-most wrapped stitches is about one-third of the original number, ending ready to work a right-side row.

WIDEN ROW: Knit to first wrapped stitch, knit first wrapped stitch without picking up the wrap, wrap the next stitch (that stitch is now wrapped twice), turn. Repeat Widen Row on right- and wrong-side rows until 1 wrapped stitch remains on each side, ready to work a right-side row.

Knit to first wrapped stitch, slip it knitwise, pick up the bar between the 2 stitches with the right needle, insert the left needle into the first 2 stitches on the right needle, and knit those 2 stitches through back loops (as if to complete an ssk); do not turn work. Resume working in the round.

Work in the round to remaining wrapped stitch, pick up the bar between the 2 stitches with the left needle, knit the wrapped stitch together with the picked-up stitch, knit to end of heel stitches. Heel is complete. Continue working in the round for the foot.

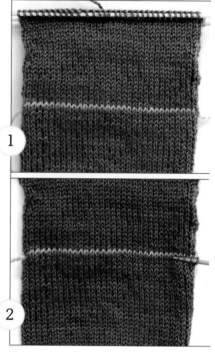

AFTERTHOUGHT HEEL

An afterthought heel can be a great choice when the heel is to be worked in a contrasting color. Sometimes, if yardage is short, it might be wise to set up for an afterthought heel, then decide whether to use a contrasting color after the rest of the sock is worked and the remaining yarn can be measured. If there isn't enough, a different yarn can be used.

The shape and fit of an afterthought heel is identical to that of a short-row heel, but an afterthought heel is worked in the round just like a wedge toe with decreases and the Kitchener stitch instead of with short-rows. Depending on which techniques you find easier to perform, you may prefer one over the other.

To set up an afterthought heel, work waste yarn into the sock as a holder for where the heel will be worked later. Switch to waste yarn (a contrasting color is best) and knit the desired number of stitches for the heel. Cut the waste yarn leaving a few inches to make sure it will not ravel. Go back and knit the waste-yarn stitches with the main yarn. This creates a line in the sock for where the heel will be inserted later [1]. Continue working in the round for at least another inch. Some knitters wait until the end of the sock to work the heel (hence the name "afterthought heel"), but I prefer to work my heel after an inch or two. Since I only use an afterthought heel when I know I want to use a contrasting color, this allows me to measure the length of the foot more easily on a top-down sock and more accurately place the beginning of the toe. If you are working an after-

thought heel because you aren't sure you have enough yarn for the heel, wait until you've finished the rest of your sock.

Once you are ready to work the heel, carefully insert a needle through the right leg of each stitch below the waste yarn [2]. You will pick up the same number of stitches as there were stitches in the placeholder.

Rotate the work and pick up stitches from above the waste yarn, again picking up the right leg [3].

There should be one extra stitch picked up above the waste yarn [4]. If there are the same number of stitches, pick up an additional stitch on the left side. Carefully remove the waste yarn by cutting it or by

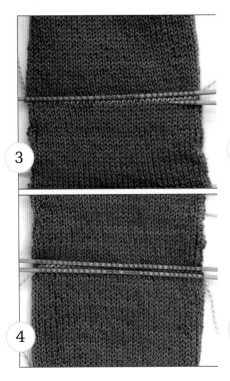

3

4

5

6

7

picking it out 1 stitch at a time.

Pick up an additional stitch at each end of each needle. Divide the stitches on top onto 2 needles with the extra stitch on the left (**5**). Number the needle with the most stitches Needle 1 and the following needles 2 and 3.

SET-UP ROUND: With new (heel) yarn, work as follows: with Needle 1, k2tog, knit to last 2 stitches, ssk (**6**); with Needle 2, k2tog twice, knit to end; with Needle 3, knit to last 2 stitches, ssk (**7**).

ROUND 1: (even round) Knit.

ROUND 2: (decrease round) K1, ssk, knit to last 3 stitches of Needle 1, k2tog, k1, knit first stitch from Needle 2, ssk, knit to last 3 stitches of Needle 3, k2tog, k1—4 stitches decreased.

Repeat Rounds 1 and 2 until heel reaches desired depth, about one-third of the number of stitches you started with. Slip stitches from Needle 3 to Needle 2. Use the Kitchener stitch (see Glossary) to graft stitches from Needles 1 and 2 together.

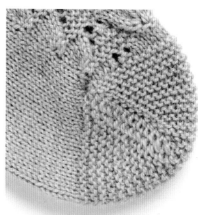

Toe Options

WEDGE TOE

A wedge toe is shaped with straight angles. It is easy to remember and provides a good fit.

Begin the toe 2" (5 cm) before desired length of foot. Mark the left and right sides of the foot, with the round beginning at the right side of the foot.

ROUND 1: (even round) Knit.

ROUND 2: (decrease round) K1, ssk, knit to 3 stitches before left side of foot, k2tog, k1, slip marker (sl m), k1, ssk, knit to 3 stitches before right side of foot, k2tog, k1—4 stitches decreased.

Repeat Rounds 1 and 2 until sock measures desired length.

Graft stitches from top of foot together with stitches from the sole using Kitchener stitch (see Glossary).

ROUND TOE

For a rounder, less pointy toe, use a round toe, which leaves a bit more room for the toe area. It is worked like the wedge toe except that instead of decreasing every other round to form a straight angle, the decrease rounds are interspersed with more even rounds. Begin the toe 1½" (3.8 cm) before desired length of foot. Even and decrease rounds are as given for Wedge Toe at left.

Work even round 4 times, then decrease round once.

Work even round 3 times, then decrease round once.

Work even round 2 times, then decrease round once.

Work even round once, then decrease round once.

Work decrease round once more.

Graft stitches from the top of foot together with stitches from the sole using Kitchener stitch (see Glossary).

SHORT-ROW TOE

A short-row toe is worked just like a short-row heel, over exactly half the stitches in the round. Once the short-rows are completed, Kitchener stitch (see Glossary) is used to graft the short-row stitches to the held stitches.

The toe shown here is short-rowed in garter stitch.

The Art of Placement

There are many ways to position stitch patterns on a sock; two socks with the same base elements can be completely different depending on placement. By rotating, mirroring, or staggering, the same elements can give very different results. When working a sock from cuff to toe, the most significant decision about placement is where the heel should fall. The general rule of thumb is to divide such that about half the stitches are used for the heel and half are used for the top of the foot. It's not essential that the numbers be exactly 50/50; sometimes it may even be preferable to divide unevenly.

1 The most common sock pattern is one that uses an even number of repeats around the leg. This makes dividing for the top of the foot and the heel easy, and many will simply divide in half and leave it at that. However, there are more options, and a generic even-repeat sock can have different variations to play with.

2 When combining multiple vertical patterns for a pattern, placement can play a pivotal role in the overall look of the sock. Here, the same vertical panels are combined in two different ways.

3 The orientation of the stitch patterns can affect the overall look as well. By mirroring the left and right socks, a pair can gain a new level of sophistication.

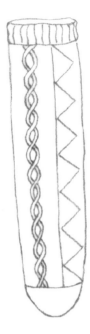

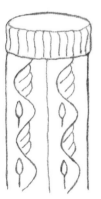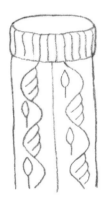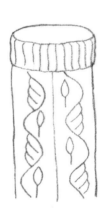

4 Elements don't have to fit into a rectangular grid; a staggered pattern might lend an interesting visual effect. Shifting the right column (center sock) creates a staggered effect. Play with mirroring and staggering the elements (right sock) to see what different combinations can be made and which best fits your vision.

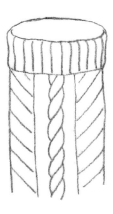 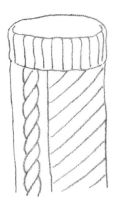 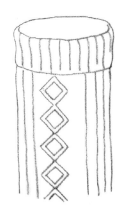

| Symmetry | Asymmetry | Awkward non-symmetry |

5 Neither symmetry nor asymmetry is better than the other, but if you choose one, make sure it shows in the design. Some patterns look as though they fall somewhere between symmetry and asymmetry, a sign that the pattern was not well planned. Whichever you choose, make sure it looks intentional.

6 Using an odd number of repeats can pose some special problems, since it will not divide evenly in half. The same stitch pattern with an odd number of repeats around the leg can be handled to yield very different results.

stitch techniques

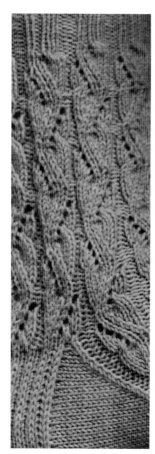

Master the Basics

To knit the socks in this book and to begin adapting or designing sock patterns, you should be comfortable with casting on, knitting in the round, slipping stitches, picking up slipped stitches, and the Kitchener stitch. These are outlined in the Glossary on pages 135–141.

In addition, a good understanding of the different parts of the sock and how they are constructed is essential. A basic sock has the following components: the leg, the heel, the top of the foot, the sole, and the toe. A sock can also have a gusset or cuff.

The most interesting parts of a sock are generally in the leg and the top of the foot. This is where texture is usually placed, and I refer to it as the main texture area. The texture can also extend to the other components of the sock, but it doesn't have to. The main texture area is knit in a complete round for the leg portion of the sock, then divided into two sections—one that will become the heel of the sock and another that will become the top of the foot. The top of the foot is a continuation of the main texture area and is no longer knit in a complete round. Instead the top of the foot is usually textured and bound on either side

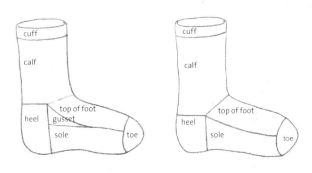

where the bottom of the foot and gusset are in smooth stockinette stitch.

The main texture covers different shapes and areas on the sock. On the leg, a stitch pattern is often knit in the round. On the top of the foot, it is also worked in the round but as a rectangle with straight edges on each side. If the pattern is continued onto a heel flap, it is worked back and forth. In order to work the same stitch pattern in different ways, it's essential to know how to convert a single stitch from right side to wrong side as well as how to convert an entire stitch pattern from flat to all over in-the-round to rectangular in-the-round and back again.

Inverting Stitches

Stockinette stitch is accomplished either by knitting all stitches in the round or by alternating knit and purl rows when working flat. Because a knit stitch is the inverse of a purl stitch, a knit stitch looks like a purl stitch when viewed from the opposite side. When working in the round, the right side is always facing and every knit stitch lies the same way, whereas flat knitting alternates between the right and wrong side every row. To achieve the same result, the inverse of the knit stitch (a purl stitch) is worked on the wrong side rows. From the right side, it looks the same as knitting all the stitches in the round.

INVERTING MULTIPLE STITCHES

When multiple stitches or a whole row must be inverted, not only does each stitch have to be inverted but the order must also be reversed, because the direction of knitting is in the opposite direction. For example, "k1, p2, k3, k2tog" becomes "p2tog, p3, k2, p1" on the reverse.

Inverse Stitches

☐	Knit		⦁	Purl
⦿	Yarnover		⦿	Yarnover
⟋	K2tog		⟋	P2tog
⟨	K3tog		⟨	P3tog
⟍	Ssk		⟍	Ssp
⟩	Sssk		⟩	Sssp
⟰	Sl 1 kwise, k2tog, psso		⟰	P2tog, slip stitch pwise from right needle to left needle, pass 2nd stitch on left needle over first stitch, slip stitch pwise from left needle to right needle

R	Make 1 (right leaning)		L·	Make 1 purlwise (left leaning)
L	Make 1 (left leaning)		R·	Make 1 purlwise (right leaning)
ℛ	K tbl		ℛ	P tbl
Ⅴ	Knit into front, back, front of same st		Ⅴ	Purl into front, back, front of same st
Ⅴ	Sl 1 wyb		Ⅴ	Sl 1 wyf

INVERTING CABLES

Any cable, no matter how complex, can be deconstructed into 4 components.

- Grouping: This is how the stitches are divided and grouped on the cable needles and left needle. The groups are lettered from left to right as A, B, C (if necessary).
- Front-to-back order: This is the order from front-most to back-most of how the groups are placed. For example, when one needle is placed to the back of the work, that group of stitches is farther back in the front-to-back order.
- Working order: This is the order in which the groups are worked. For example, if there is one cable needle the stitches from the left needle (Group A) are worked first, then the stitches from the cable needle (Group B).
- Stitches per group: This is the actual stitches to be performed on each group.

Simple cable example:

Place 2 stitches onto cable needle and move to back of work. K2 from left needle. K2 from cable needle.

Deconstructing, we get:

The stitches are grouped with 2 stitches on the left needle and 2 stitches on the cable needle. We label these groupings A and B.

The front-to-back order of the groups is A, B; Group A is in front of Group B.

The working order is A, B; the stitches in Group A are worked before the stitches in Group B.

The stitches in both groups are worked as k2.

From this, we can create a diagram, and by rotating the diagram to get an opposite side perspective we can determine the inverse of the cable.

Interpreting the rotated diagram from right to left, we get the inverse: Place 2 stitches on cable needle (Group A) and hold in back of work (Group B is in front). P2 (the inverse of k2) from left needle (Group B is worked first). P2 (the inverse of k2) from cable needle (Group A is worked second).

Complex cable example:

Place 4 stitches onto Cable Needle 1 and move to back of work. Place 5 stitches onto Cable Needle 2 and move to front of work. K2, p3, k1 from left needle. K2, p2 from Cable Needle 1. K2, p2, k1 from Cable Needle 2.

Deconstructing, we get:

The stitches are distributed from left to right: 6 stitches on the left needle, 5 stitches on Cable Needle 2, and 4 stitches on Cable Needle 1. We can label these groups from left to right as A, B, and C.

The front-to-back order of the groups is B, A, C.

The working order is A, C, B.

Simple cable:

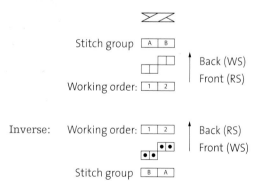

Complex cable:

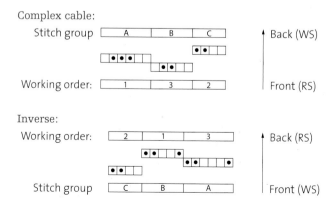

The stitches are worked: Group A as k2, p3, k1; Group B as k2, p2, k1; and Group C as k2, p2.

To figure out the inverse, rotate the diagram to see how the groups are affected. The group from left to right on the right side was A, B, C, but on the wrong side it is reversed to C, B, A. The group that was the front-most is now the back-most and vice versa. The working order is also reversed; instead of A, C, B, it will be worked B, C, A. For each grouping, the stitches will be worked with opposite-side directions.

So the inverse of the example cable is: Place 6 stitches on Cable Needle 1 (Group A) and place in back of work (Group C is in front of Group A). Place 5 stitches on Cable Needle 2 (this is Group B) and place in back of work behind Cable Needle 2 (Group B is the back-most group). P1, k2, p2 (this is the inverse of k2, p2, k1) from Cable Needle 2 (Group B is worked first). K2, p2 (this is the inverse of p2, k2) from left needle (Group C is worked second). P1, k3, p2 (this is the inverse of k2, p3, k1) from Cable Needle 1 (Group A is worked third).

INVERTING OTHER COMPLEX STITCHES

Other complicated stitch patterns can span more than one stitch. To invert stitches like this, deconstruct them into their components and reverse. The components of multi-stitch patterns are similar to cables:

- Grouping
- Working order
- Stitch manipulation

To invert the stitch, we reverse the grouping and the stitch manipulation only; unlike with cables, the working order remains the same. The nature of cables is to reverse stitch order by swapping stitches left or right directionally, so the directional order must be reversed on the opposite side. For non-cable stitches, the working order is not directional, because each step is dependent on the previous one.

If you understand things better visually, it's probably easiest to try to do each step on the right side and rotate your knitting around to see how that looks from the opposite side. Then try to replicate that on the other side. Always double check to make sure your stitch looks correct on the right side.

	With RS facing	With WS facing
	Cable 1K R 1K	Cable 1P R 1P
	Cable 2K R 2K	Cable 2P R 2P
	Cable 3K R 3K	Cable 3P R 3P
	Cable 1K L 1K	Cable 1P L 1P
	Cable 2K L 2K	Cable 2P L 2P
	Cable 3K L 3K	Cable 3P L 3P
	Cable 1K R 1P	Cable 1K R 1P
	Cable 2K R 1P	Cable 1K R 2P
	Cable 3K R 1P	Cable 1K R 3P
	Cable 1P L 1K	Cable 1P L 1K
	Cable 1P L 2K	Cable 2P L 1K
	Cable 1P L 3K	Cable 3P L 1K
	Cable 1K tbl R 1K tbl	Cable 1P tbl R 1P tbl
	Cable 2K tbl R 2K tbl	Cable 2P tbl R 2P tbl
	Cable 3K tbl R 3K tbl	Cable 3P tbl R 3P tbl
	Cable 1K tbl L 1K tbl	Cable 1P tbl L 1P tbl
	Cable 2K tbl L 2K tbl	Cable 2P tbl L 2P tbl
	Cable 3K tbl L 3K tbl	Cable 3P tbl L 3P tbl
	Cable 1K tbl R 1P	Cable 1K R 1P tbl
	Cable 2K tbl R 1P	Cable 1K R 2P tbl
	Cable 3K tbl R 1P	Cable 1K R 3P tbl
	Cable 1P L 1K tbl	Cable 1P tbl L 1K
	Cable 1P L 2K tbl	Cable 2P tbl L 1K
	Cable 1P L 3K tbl	Cable 3P tbl L 1K

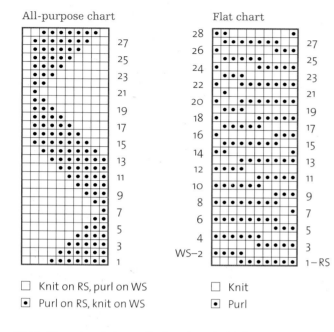

All-purpose chart

| | 27 |
| 25 |
| 23 |
| 21 |
| 19 |
| 17 |
| 15 |
| 13 |
| 11 |
| 9 |
| 7 |
| 5 |
| 3 |
| 1 |

Flat chart

28	
26	27
24	25
22	23
20	21
18	19
16	17
14	15
12	13
10	11
8	9
6	7
4	5
WS–2	3
	1–RS

☐ Knit on RS, purl on WS
▣ Purl on RS, knit on WS

☐ Knit
▣ Purl

Which of these charts looks more like the socks on the right?

Working with Charts

When working with complex stitch patterns, it is easier for both the designer and the knitter to work from charts rather than written-out directions . . . as long as the chart is truly representative of the knitting.

ALL-PURPOSE VS FLAT KNITTING CHARTS

Not all knitting charts are the same. It is common to have one symbol that means "knit on the right side, purl on the wrong side," and charts with this type of key are designed for all-purpose knitting—when in the round, you work every row from right to left (just as you are knitting from right to left) and read every symbol as though you are on the right side, ignoring the wrong-side instructions. When working flat, you alternate reading from right to left and from left to right with every row, just as you knit back and forth across the piece in different directions; the right-side instructions are used when reading from right to left, and the wrong-side instructions are used when reading from left to right.

There are also charts that are designed specifically for flat knitting. These are read alternating left to right then right to left, but the knitter does not have to convert any symbols for right side or wrong side since it is done in the chart. While it may seem more convenient to use this type of chart, these charts are less representative of what the knitted fabric will look like on the right side and require conversion to in-the-round directions for socks.

CONVERTING A FLAT CHART TO AN ALL-PURPOSE CHART

All-purpose charts are a must for sock design because socks are worked in the round. To convert a flat chart to an all-purpose chart, convert each symbol on each wrong-side row to its inverse.

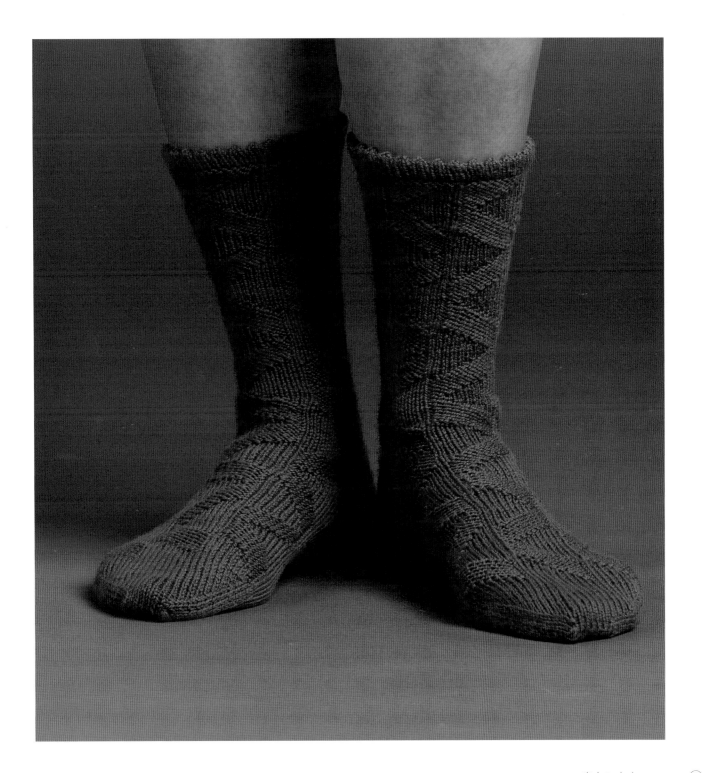

CHARTING A WRITTEN-FOR-FLAT PATTERN

Flat patterns are usually written for a multiple of stitches plus some. For example, a stitch pattern might be a multiple of X stitches plus Y. Because flat knitting has clear edges on each side, the additional Y stitches are used for the edges. To get a good feel for the pattern and where the edge begins and ends, chart out two full repeats plus the additional Y stitches.

ROW 1: (WS) P3, *ssp, yo, p3, yo, p2tog, p5; repeat from *, ending with p3.
ROW 2: (RS) K2, *k2tog, yo, k5, yo, ssk, k3; repeat from *, ending with k2.
ROW 3: (WS) P1, *ssp, yo, p7, yo, p2tog, p1; repeat from *.
ROW 4: (RS) K2tog, *yo, k2, k2tog, yo, k1, yo, ssk, k2, yo, sl1, k2tog, psso; repeat from * to last 2 stitches, ssk.
(Multiple of 12 stitches + 1)

1. Create a grid that is Y plus twice X squares wide and the appropriate number of rows tall.

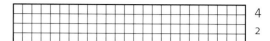

2. Fill in the first row from left to right because it is a wrong-side row, using the inverse symbols (see page 25) and charting the repeat section twice. P3 becomes three knit squares because knit is the inverse of purl.

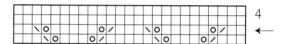

3. Fill in the second row from right to left because it is a right-side row, using the appropriate symbols, again charting the repeat section twice.

Common Charting Errors

COMMON MISTAKE 1: CHARTING ONLY FROM * TO *

Since the repeat in the round will be X stitches without the extra Y stitches, it may be tempting to create a chart that is X stitches wide and only chart from the repeat section in the written pattern. However, written directions are written in such a way that the number of stitches before the repeat do not necessarily correspond with the edge stitches. For example, if we had charted only the repeat section in the example, this would have been the resulting chart.

See how the rows are not aligned properly because the number of stitches before and after each * in the written directions does not stay constant. This offsets the pattern.

COMMON MISTAKE 2: CHARTING ONLY ONE REPEAT

It can be difficult to see how many stitches are used for the edges and which stitches those are. Only by charting a full two repeats can we determine the difference between edge stitches and repeat stitches. If we had charted only one repeat in the example, Row 4 would have been misrepresented.

By charting only one pattern repeat's width (13 stitches), the entire * to * section in Row 4 is not charted and the double decrease is left out.

4. Continue filling out the rows back and forth until the grid has been filled.

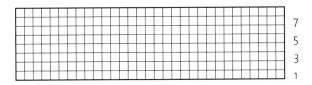

CHARTING A WRITTEN-FOR-FLAT PATTERN WITH VARYING WIDTH

Some patterns do not keep a consistent stitch count throughout. One row may have 11 stitches, then increase to 13 stitches, then decrease back to 11 stitches. In this case, the grid should be widened to accommodate the widest row, and some squares in the grid will represent "no stitch."

ROW 1: (RS) *K1, yo, k8, yo; repeat from *, k1.
(Multiple of 9 + 1 increased to Multiple of 11 + 1)
ROW 2: (WS) *K2, p8, k1; repeat from *, k1.
(Multiple of 11 + 1)
ROW 3: *K2, yo, k8, yo, k1; repeat from *, k1.
(Multiple of 11 + 1 increased to Multiple of 13 + 1)
ROW 4: *K3, p8, k2; repeat from *, k1.
(Multiple of 13 + 1)
ROW 5: *K3, yo, k8, yo, k2; repeat from *, k1.
(Multiple of 13 + 1 increased to Multiple of 15 + 1)
ROW 6: *K4, p8, k3; repeat from *, k1.
(Multiple of 15 + 1)
ROW 7: *K4, ssskp, k4tog, k3; repeat from *, k1.
(Multiple of 15 + 1 decreased to Multiple of 9 +1)
ROW 8: Knit. (Multiple of 9 + 1)

1. To chart this example, we look at the widest row, a multiple of 15 + 1. The grid should be 31 stitches wide (twice 15 plus 1).

2. Start by charting the widest rows. Note that in this pattern, the odd-numbered rows are RS rows and the even-numbered rows are WS rows. Row 5 is filled in from right to left into the grid; Row 6 is filled in from left to right into the grid and by inverting each stitch.

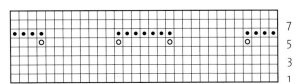

3. We can work our way down row by row, beginning with Row 4. Whenever the row below has fewer stitches than the row above, there must be increases without corresponding decreases in the row above. Mark the squares in the chart underneath those increases as "no stitch." Row 4 has fewer stitches than Row 5, and the yarnovers in Row 5 do not have corresponding decreases, so we mark those as "no stitch." Then fill in the row below, skipping the "no stitch" squares. Row 4 is a wrong-side row, so it is filled in from left to right and by inverting each stitch. Continue working down until the narrowest row has been filled.

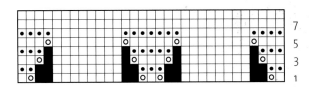

■ no stitch

4. We then begin working our way up from the widest row. If the row above has fewer stitches than the row below, there must be a decrease on the row above with no corresponding increase. Determine which stitches are being decreased from the row below and mark them as "no stitch." For example, Row 7 has fewer stitches than Row 6. Row 7 has two triple decreases without corresponding increases — the ssskp and k4tog. Each decrease eliminates 3 stitches. On Row 7, we fill in each stitch from right to left. Because the ssskp takes 4 knit stitches from the row below in order to perform it, we put the

ssskp into one square and mark the three other squares above the worked stitches below as no stitch. Similarly, the k4tog is placed into one square and three squares are marked as no stitch. We can fill in the rows above this way until the entire grid has been filled.

⚔ k4tog

⚔ ssskp

CONVERTING A WRITTEN-FOR-FLAT PATTERN TO ALLOVER IN-THE-ROUND

Flat patterns often include border stitches that are unnecessary in the round. To work an all-purpose chart seamlessly in the round, we must isolate the pattern repeat without border stitches. The beginning of the round can pose special problems. In particular, stitch patterns with decreases or cables at the edges can be tricky to handle.

If we have just charted the pattern ourselves, the first step is to isolate the pattern repeat. Remember, if the pattern repeat is marked as a multiple of X plus Y stitches, in the round it will be a multiple of X stitches only. For the easiest stitch patterns, we can create an outline rectangle that is X stitches wide by R rows tall (where R is the number of rows in the pattern repeat). It is best to place the repeat box in such a way that it doesn't cut any lines in the pattern. Cutting a pattern line—whether created by increases, decreases, or cables—usually creates a visible jog at the beginning of the round and should be avoided whenever possible. If there are tricky edge stitches to handle, the box may become a different shape.

The following examples illustrate how to determine the placement of the repeat box and how to handle some of the challenges of tricky edge situations.

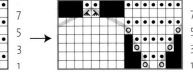

1 This stitch pattern is straightforward after isolating the repeat section. The pattern repeat box could be shifted to the left or right, but the placement chosen avoids splitting the lines created by the yarnovers. Once we've placed the pattern repeat box, working allover in the round is just a matter of repeating the stitch pattern.

Lines formed by yarnovers

Lines formed by decreases

2 Again, we place the pattern repeat box in a way that avoids splitting any of the lines created by the decreases or increases. While this stitch pattern appears simple, the decrease at the edge (highlighted in yellow) will cause problems because it requires using a stitch from the end of the previous repeat as well as from the beginning of the current repeat. Because this stitch pattern only has patterning on every other row, we can "borrow" a stitch (highlighted in blue) from the plain round before it. By ending the previous round one stitch early, we leave the last stitch in that round for the double decrease at the beginning of the current round.

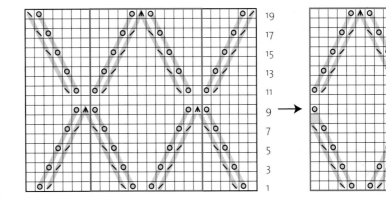

3 This stitch pattern is exactly the same as Example 2, but there are no plain rows. We can't "borrow" a plain stitch from the end of the previous round because the last stitch in the previous round is itself a decrease. Incorporate the newly formed decrease from the end of the previous round (highlighted in blue) into our decrease at the beginning of the current round.

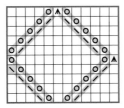

Ⓐ Double decrease except at the beginning of round— k2tog, pass last stitch from previous round over new stitch.

□ This stitch is "borrowed" to complete the double decrease at the beginning of the next round.

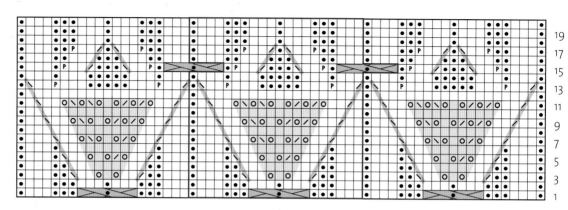

19
17
15
13
11
9
7
5
3
1

4 No matter how we shift the box here, we will interrupt the lace area or cables. If given the choice to interrupt cables or lace, it is usually easier to handle cable edge stitches than lace edge stitches. Instead of splitting the pattern where the cables occur, we create a jog in our repeat section. To work the cable, we can borrow stitches from the previous round as we did in Example 2. This shortens the round before and must be marked.

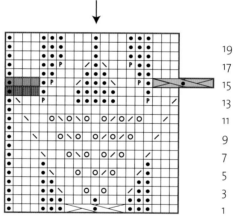

19
17
15
13
11
9
7
5
3
1

These sts are included in the pattern rep, BUT omit these sts from the last rep and end rnd early, shifting beg of rnd to the right.

These sts are NOT included in the pattern rep. Work these sts at the end of rnd only, shifting beg of rnd to the left.

Cable

Lace area

Lines formed by decreases

5 Diagonal stitch patterns can pose problems if you try to force them into a rectangular repeat. To avoid splitting any of the lines, the best way to handle a diagonal stitch pattern is to outline on the diagonal. This is similar to the jogs associated with decreases at the edges, except there is a decrease at every edge, so the jogs end up continual and on the diagonal. While this stitch pattern looks like it is jogging, there is no need to switch stitches around on the needles. The decreases at the beginning of the round and the increases at the end of the round naturally lend to the diagonal leaning.

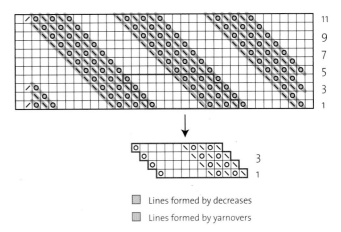

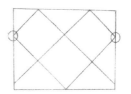

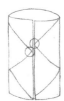

Lines formed by decreases
Lines formed by yarnovers

6 Stitch patterns with diamonds can be the most difficult. The reason for this is clear if you draw a diamond grid on a piece of paper and then try to join it into the round. Because knitting in the round is actually a spiral, the vertices of the diamond lattice become offset, and a seam is apparent. To minimize this effect, the stitch pattern repeat should be chosen carefully so that the jog is in the least visible location.

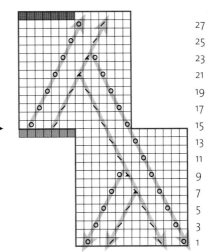

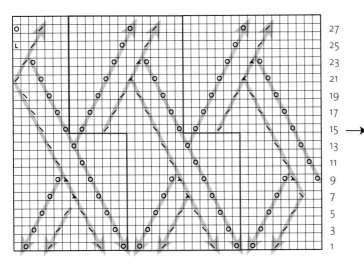

7 This is another example of a lattice-type pattern, except the lines here are created by cables instead of paired increases and decreases. Again, to avoid a visible jog, we try to create a repeat shape that does not split any of the lines. If jogs are needed, place them away from the cables if possible. Also, when cables occur every other round, make sure a plain round is maintained between cables —avoid creating a jog that leads to a cable immediately above another cable without a plain row in between. Sometimes a visible jog is inevitable, but do your best to avoid it.

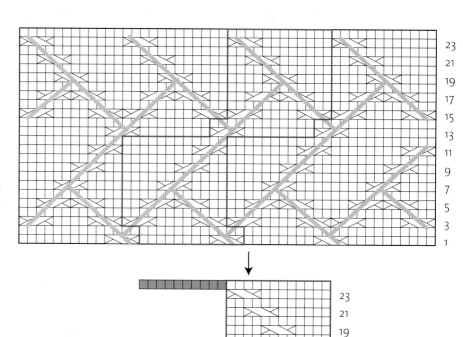

☐ Lines formed by cables

▦ These sts are included in the pattern rep, BUT omit these sts from the last rep and end rnd early, shifting beg of rnd to the right.

▨ These sts are NOT included in the pattern rep.
Work these sts at the end of rnd only, shifting beg of rnd to the left.

CONVERTING ALLOVER IN-THE-ROUND TO RECTANGULAR

As we can see from the previous examples, stitch patterns knitted allover in-the-round are often not rectangular. Confining an allover in-the-round pattern to a rectangle can involve some finesse. Some things to keep in mind are:

- Should the edges be well defined, or should they blend into the background?
- Where should the edges be placed?
- Do additional increases or decreases need to be added to maintain a consistent stitch count?
- Should additional stitches be added to the edges?

First, isolate the area you want to use for the rectangle. Pay special attention to the width and the stitches at the edges. Sometimes it will make sense to go a little wider or narrower to get the right visual affect. The bottom of the rectangle is also important.

The following examples illustrate some of the challenges and options in converting a flat chart to be worked in the round.

1 This stitch pattern is fairly straightforward. The rectangle is deliberately chosen to include purl lines on both sides. Since the background for the bottom of the foot is in stockinette, the purl lines will provide definition to the edges.

2 This stitch pattern is also fairly straightforward but differs from the one above. The edges are not well defined and blend into the stockinette background of the rest of the sock. There are also a few edge stitches to handle. The double decreases at the beginning of the round result in some stitch count mischief. These must be converted to single decreases in order to keep the stitch count correct. Note that by widening the rectangle a bit in one direction, an interesting asymmetry is achieved.

Added purls for symmetry

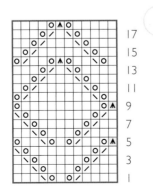

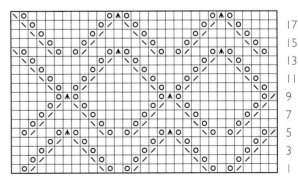

Half repeat

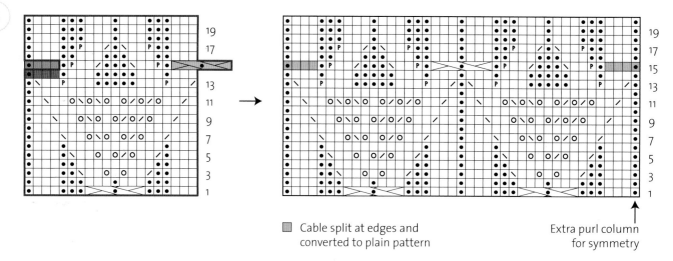

3

Cable split at edges and
converted to plain pattern

Extra purl column
for symmetry

3 Cable jogs at the beginning of the round can lead to interesting rectangles. Creating a rectangle large enough so that none of the cables needs to be split doesn't look as appealing as simply cutting some cables down the middle. These are converted to plain stitches without cabling.

4 Diagonal patterns are always fun but challenging. In this lace lattice pattern, special care was taken to make sure the stitch counts added up after each row. Make sure every decrease has a corresponding increase and vice versa. Increases and decreases were added to Rows 7, 9, 11, and 13 to maintain the decrease and increase lines. On Rows

7 and 9, the stitches at the edges were changed from double decreases to single decreases to maintain proper stitch count. Even though the stitch counts would have added up on Row 11, the placement of the lines would have shifted without the addition of an increase at the beginning and a decrease at the end.

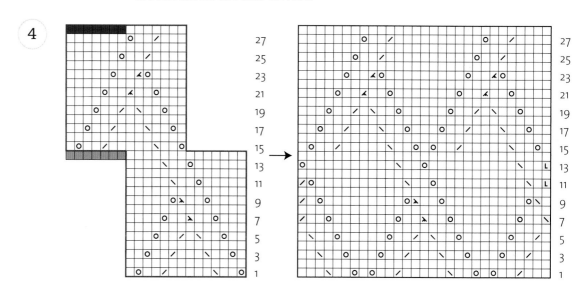

4

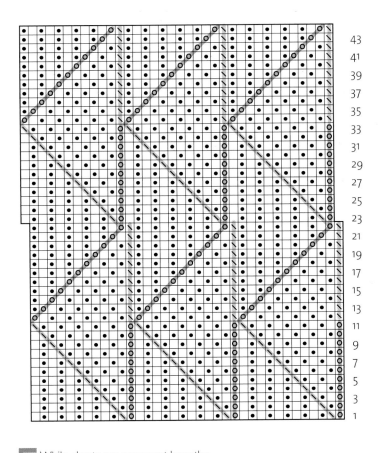

43
41
39
37
35
33
31
29
27
25
23
21
19
17
15
13
11
9
7
5
3
1

5 While charts can represent how the final work will look, sometimes a chart won't look exactly like the knitted fabric. The highlighted lines over the photo correspond to the highlighted lines in the chart—note these are not the same shape. Only by looking at the knitted sample can we see the problem that will arise when trying conform this pattern to a rectangle. The scalloped edges are jagged. To create a smoother edge, we have to lessen the jaggedness (see orange line in photo above right) by playing with the chart.

MIRRORING

Mirroring a stitch pattern is often used in sock knitting so that the right and left socks are mirror images of each other. It can also be used to mirror elements within a single sock. Some stitches are directional, meaning if you held a mirror up to it the reflected image would not be the same. Here is a chart indicating what the mirror images of some stitches are. Note that many stitches are the mirror images of themselves.

To mirror an entire chart, reverse the order of each row and replace each symbol with its mirror image. Or, since directional stitch symbols and their mirrored counterparts are usually the mirror images of each other, you can often get away with reflecting the chart itself. For example, reflecting the diagonal stitch pattern below results in the mirror image.

Mirror Table

R·	M1P-R		**L·**	M1P-L
R	M1R		**L**	M1L
⟋	K2tog		⟍	Ssk
⟋	K3tog		⟍	Sssk
⟋	P2tog		⟍	Ssp
⟋	P3tog		⟍	Sssp
	Cable 1K R 1K			Cable 1K L 1K
	Cable 1K R 1P			Cable 1P L 1K
	Cable 1Ktbl R 1Ktbl			Cable 1Ktbl L 1Ktbl
	Cable 2K R 1K			Cable 1K L 2K
	Cable 2K R 1P			Cable 1P L 2K
	Cable 2K R 2K			Cable 2K L 2K
	Cable 2K R 2P			Cable 2P L 2K
	Cable 3K R 3K			Cable 3K L 3K
	Cable 3K R 3P			Cable 3P L 3K

Exact self-inverses:

☐	Knit
●	Purl
O	Yarnover
Ѷ	Kfbf
Ѷ	Kfbfbf
V	Slip 1 st pwise

Approximate self-inverses*:

Ꙡ	K tbl
Ꙡ	P tbl
Ѷ	Kfbfb
M	Make 1
P	Make 1 purlwise

Mirrored chart

* For most purposes, these stitches can be used as their own inverses. For some twisted-stitch patterns or others that require exact mirror imaging, an exact mirror may be needed. For example, to exactly mirror K tbl, the stitch would need to be twisted in the opposite direction by slipping the stitch kwise to the right needle, back to the left needle, and then knitting as normal.

How Stitches Affect the Knitted Fabric

Choosing stitch patterns can get the creative juices flowing or it can be daunting. With so many options, how can you pick the perfect one? There are several things to keep in mind—different types of stitches affect the knitted fabric differently. Some are more elastic, some are thicker, and some work better with variegated yarns. These factors are important when considering fit or estimating the number of stitches needed.

Ribbing draws in and is quite elastic. The wider each ribbed section, the more the fabric draws in. Twisted stitches are slightly less elastic than regular stitches but are still more elastic than stockinette. They also have a different visual impact because twisted stitches pop out more.

Biased stitches or stitches that are knitted at an angle require more stitches to get the same width. They are great for working with multicolored yarns, where the color variation is highlighted by the angles of biased knitting.

Cables are overlaps in the knitted fabric, so they require more stitches for the same width. They are also bulkier and provide lots of warmth.

Stranded knitting is a great choice for cold weather because it is thick, but it is not very elastic.

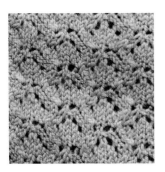

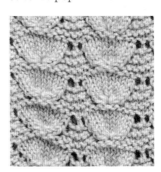

Increases and decreases remove elasticity from the fabric because they combine multiple stitches into one or create extra stitches where there weren't any before. Any stitch pattern that has a lot of increases and decreases will have less elasticity than one that doesn't. For this reason, some chevron and lace patterns can be particularly inelastic.

Purl stitches can be looser than knit stitches, depending on the knitter. This can be evident when working knit/purl combination stitches or garter stitch in the round; the purl sections may end up looser than the knitted sections.

Lace can be holey and inelastic if the fabric is too open, or it can stretch out quite a bit, so it's important to block lace before measuring fit.

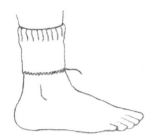
Perfect fit around the leg

Too baggy around the leg

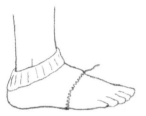
Make sure the sock can fit over the heel

Too tight to go around the heel

THE IMPORTANCE OF ELASTICITY

To put on a sock, you must pull the top section over your heel. Because the heel area can be bigger than the ankle, this can be a problem area for fit. The key to this is elasticity. If the fit is snug around the leg portion of the sock, it may not fit over the heel if the fabric is not elastic enough. If the leg portion is made wide enough to fit over the heel, it might be too loose and baggy to stay up straight on the leg. Combine elastic components with inelastic components to improve overall fit.

CABLES

Cables can use up quite a bit of yarn because the crossing of the stitches draws in the width of the fabric. Knitters may cable more or less tightly than others, so trying to guess how wide a cable pattern will be involves a bit of voodoo science. The factors that determine the amount of draw-in within a cable pattern are the types of cables used and the spacing between the cables.

An individual cable is as wide as the average of the sections it is crossing. For example, if a cable crosses 3 stitches over 3 stitches, the overlap will happen evenly and the width is 3 stitches. If a cable crosses 3 stitches over 1 stitch, the average width is 2 stitches. Complex cables that cross multiple groups are averaged in the same way. Crossing three groups of 2, 4, and 4 stitches results in an average width of 3⅓ stitches. The average numbers here assume a tight cable cross. If you cable loosely (if you notice a ladder to the right or the left of your cables), then your cables may be a little wider.

A cable pattern that has cabling on every row will be denser and narrower than the same pattern with extra uncabled rows. The number of rows or rounds between the cables affects the width of the piece. The more space, the more relaxed the fabric and the more it will stretch. In particular, cables that spiral around are more constricting than cables in a vertical line.

The more rows between cable crossings, the wider the cable is.

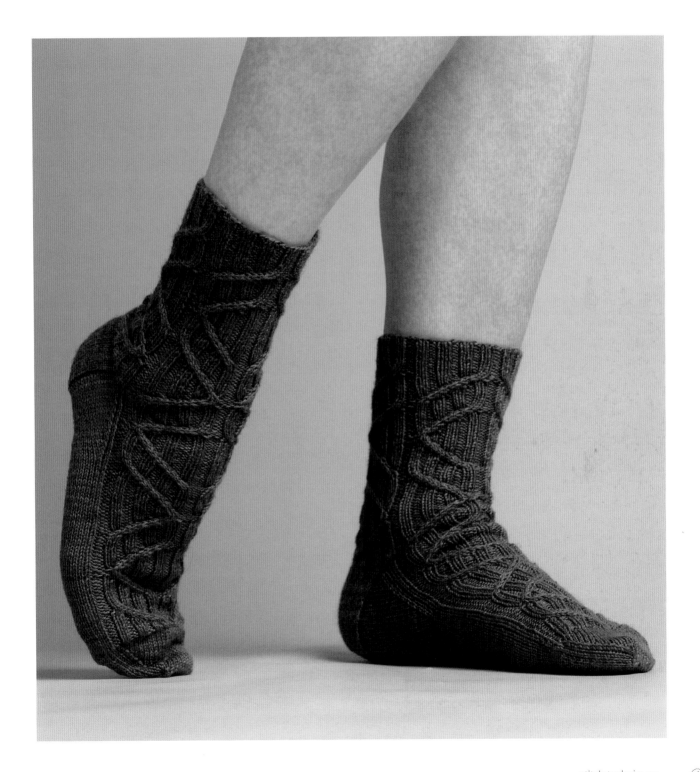

STITCH PATTERNS FOR MULTICOLORED YARN

Choosing a stitch pattern for multicolored yarns is difficult because the color variation and pooling can obscure patterning. Some people like this effect, while others try to avoid it. Biased stitches tend to show off color variation very well, while the visual prominence of twisted stitches can be used to show off a stitch pattern better. A combination of twisted and biased stitches can be very striking.

While the best way to determine a stitch pattern's effect on gauge is to knit a swatch, experimentation and experience can help you make a good guess.

Adjusting Stitch Patterns to Fit Your Needs

Sometimes a stitch pattern just doesn't quite work out how you want it. Perhaps it is too narrow, too wide, too inelastic, or just not quite the right texture. Learning to adjust stitch patterns will give you more control over what you can do with them. With practice, you'll be on your way to creating your own stitch patterns.

ISOLATING THE MAIN ELEMENTS OF A STITCH PATTERN

Before trying to make any modifications to a stitch pattern, it's necessary to isolate the main elements. Generally, you'll want to keep the essence of the stitch pattern intact. I tend to think of the main outlines within the stitch pattern and the textures within each area. Some elements are background, some are themselves lines that follow a particularly shaped path throughout the pattern, and some are foreground texture. Here are some examples of stitch patterns and their main elements.

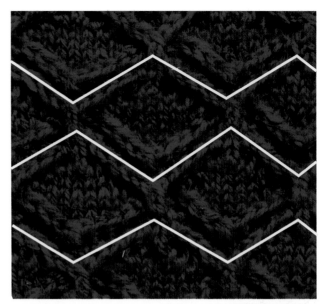

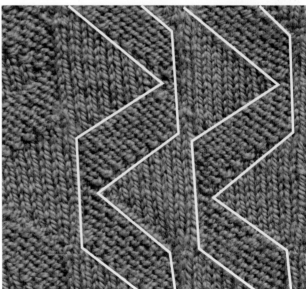

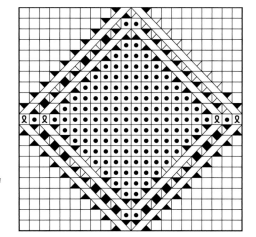

The area inside the diamond is changed from a cabled texture to reverse stockinette.

CHANGING THE TEXTURE WITHIN ONE ELEMENT OF A STITCH PATTERN

Sometimes a stitch pattern just won't be elastic enough. To add some elasticity, you may want to substitute one of the textures with ribbing, which is more elastic. Isolate the main elements and choose one that can be altered.

Alternatively, perhaps a stitch pattern is just too busy. It might make sense to convert one or more of the main elements to stockinette or reverse stockinette stitch (above). Playing with the textures can lead to many possibilities!

RESIZING A STITCH PATTERN

Most stitch patterns can be resized in a variety of ways. It helps to deconstruct the stitch pattern into smaller components. Note the lines formed by decreases and increases as well as the shapes created by the different textures. Changing the width of a pattern will often require changing the length of the pattern as well, particularly if there are diagonal components. Components are often interconnected—depending on how one component lines up with another, it's possible that changing the width of one component will require changing the width of others to match it. Also pay attention to symmetry; adding or removing a stitch on one side may require adding a second stitch to the opposite side, meaning that a pattern can only be altered by two stitches at a time.

1 We can see in the photo of this stitch pattern that the shape is a diamond. By connecting the increases to each other (like connecting dots) and then connecting the decreases with different-colored lines, the connection between the knitted fabric and the chart becomes clear. To widen the chart, extend each line outward by 1 stitch, adding 2 stitches total to the repeat. The pattern is also lengthened by 2 rows. Widening 1 line by 1 stitch requires widening each of the lines by a stitch, but the pattern is symmetrical both horizontally and vertically. The diagonal lines also require us to lengthen the chart.

2 This stitch pattern is more complicated, but the same approach applies. First, create the increase and decrease lines. Then shade in the different textures within the pattern: the lace trapezoid shape (orange) and the purl sections (green). To widen this pattern, enlarge the lace shape and the center purl region. For symmetry, we have to widen by 2 stitches. This also requires widening the 4 other purl regions.

Alternatively, we could have widened the knit sections instead of the purl sections. However, since the knit sections lead into one another, this would require adding 4 stitches to the width (possibly too much for our needs). Also, since the cable crosses the 2 knit regions, we would have to widen the cable.

1

2

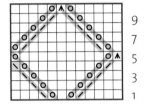

9
7
5
3
1

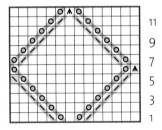

11
9
7
5
3
1

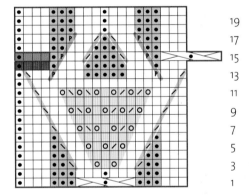

19
17
15
13
11
9
7
5
3
1

□ Purl area

□ Lace area

▨ Lines formed by decreases

▨ Lines formed by increases

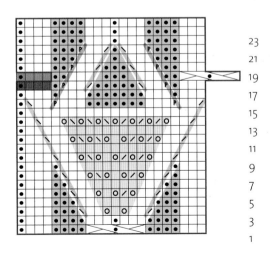

23
21
19
17
15
13
11
9
7
5
3
1

Cable increases and decreases

TRANSITIONING FROM ONE STITCH PATTERN TO ANOTHER

At key areas of the sock, particularly at the cuff and toe and perhaps at the heel, a transition will need to be made from ribbing or stockinette to a stitch pattern (or vice versa). If the stitch patterns have a different gauge, increases or decreases will be necessary to keep the transition smooth.

1 When transitioning from a cabled stitch pattern to stockinette (or ribbing), the cables should be decreased to prevent puckering from the excess fabric. To decrease in a cable pattern, put stitches on the cable needle as normal. Instead of working the cable as usual, decrease stitches by knitting them together from the left needle and the cable needle.

2 When transitioning from stockinette (or ribbing) into cables, increases can help the fabric maintain its width. There are several different methods for increasing into cables; depending on the width of the cable, one type may be more appropriate than the other (see charts below).

For narrower cables, increase by knitting into the front and back loops (or vice versa, depending on the direction of the cable).

For wider cables, use an increase set-up row before the first cable row. If the cable goes to the left, the increase goes on the left; if the cable goes to the right, the increase goes on the right.

Cables in the leg pattern are decreased to flow into foot and heel.

Cable Increase Charts

3 Transitioning from a rib to pattern is a great place to showcase attention to detail. Choose a rib that will flow seamlessly into the pattern. For example, see how the ribs above flow into the stitch patterns. Sometimes you will want to carry the ribbing into a few rows of the pattern to make the transition even smoother. If increases or decreases are needed, they should also be placed strategically within the pattern.

Once you've mastered transitioning between ribbing and stitch patterns or stockinette and stitch patterns, transitioning between two different stitch patterns will come easily. The same general rules apply: Line up elements, increase or decrease as necessary, and make the transition over multiple rows if that will smooth the transition.

COMBINING MULTIPLE STITCH PATTERNS

After you've worked with a lot of different stitch patterns and gotten more comfortable with how they work, you're ready for more advanced stitchery—a step toward creating your own stitch patterns. By taking elements from different stitch patterns, you can combine them into new patterns that suit your needs. Or think outside the box and create your own lines, then fill them in with different textures.

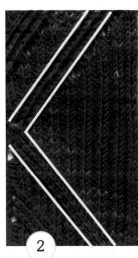

1 This pattern is a combination of three different stitch patterns arranged in a staggered formation. Each element by itself is fairly simple, but put together, the sum of the parts creates a richer whole.

2 For the top of this foot, one stitch pattern has been combined with its mirror image and with ribbing. The elements naturally lead to triangle shapes, so the boundary between elements is well defined.

sock design

At the Drawing Board

Some designers prefer to begin at the drawing board, some like to begin by choosing stitch patterns, and some go back and forth. By starting at the drawing board, you might let your imagination guide you with shapes and lines, general textures, and pattern placement. It can be as simple or complex as you choose. Generally, I begin by determining my main texture area, figure out what stitch patterns I will fill the space with, then choose coordinating heels, toes, and cuffs. At each step, I refine my sketch until I get something that represents the final design.

At the very least, before beginning a sock, you'll need to have a plan for the cuff, the main stitch pattern around the leg of the sock, and the transition from the cuff to the leg.

As you knit your sock, you'll probably learn more about the stitches you're using and how they work together. This can give you ideas that will change the sock from how you originally planned it. Keep an open mind and always think ahead. It's not uncommon to go back to the drawing board a few times before settling on a final plan.

The Gauge Swatch

As with all knitting design, you can't escape a little arithmetic. If you've knit a few basic stockinette socks before, you'll have an idea of how many stitches you normally cast on for a sock using fingering-weight yarn and your favorite needles. If not, there are ways to fudge this.

First, ignore the suggested gauge on your ball band. If you are an average knitter (not too tight, not too loose) with an average foot size (U.S. women's size 8) knitting your average fingering-weight sock yarn (some are thinner or thicker than others) using U.S. size 1 (2.25 mm) needles, 64 stitches is just about right. Of course, most of us are not average in all things.

- If you are a tight/loose knitter, you may need more/fewer stitches.
- If your ankle size is bigger/smaller, you may need more/fewer stitches.
- If your foot is wider/narrower, you may need more/fewer stitches.
- If your yarn is thinner/thicker than average, you may need more/fewer stitches.
- If your needles are smaller/bigger, you may need more/fewer stitches.

The idea is to come up with a *Target Stockinette Number* (TSN). From there, we go to the drawing board and sketch out a basic plan for how we want the sock to look. After selecting stitch patterns, we can use our knowledge of the effect of stitch patterns on the knitted fabric to calculate a *Target Pattern Number* (TPN), or the target number of stitches in pattern. These numbers will be used to begin a gauge swatch. The gauge swatch will look surprisingly just like the beginning of a sock. If you are lucky, the fit of the gauge sock will be spot on, and you can continue on your merry way to finish your sock. If you are not so lucky, you'll have to take careful notes on the fit of the gauge swatch to adjust it. The worst thing that can happen is that your gauge swatch will be just that, so don't fret the calculations.

TARGET PATTERN NUMBER

If your main stitch pattern uses multicolored stranded knitting or a lot of biased stitches, add about 10% to your TSN to count for inelasticity. (For example, if your TSN is 64 stitches, your TPN will be 70 stitches.)

If your main stitch pattern uses a lot of cables, calculate the number of stitches that are lost to cables (see page 42) on the most cable-intensive round and add this to your TSN.

If your main stitch pattern is lacy without balancing elastic components such as ribbing, subtract 10% from your TSN. For example, if your TSN is 64 stitches, your TPN will be 58 stitches.

ACTUAL PATTERN NUMBER

The APN is the actual number of stitches you will have in pattern. This can be off from your TPN by about half an inch before you'll run into fit problems. For example, if your stockinette gauge is 8 stitches per inch, you have a 4-stitch leeway for your APN and TPN to differ. Once the APN and TPN differ by more than 4 stitches, you'll have to make changes for the sock to fit.

For example, if:
Main stitch pattern repeat = 8 stitches.
TPN = 60 stitches.
Stockinette gauge = 8 st/in.
Then:
7 repeats of the main stitch pattern is 56 stitches; 8 repeats is 64 stitches. Both are only 4 stitches off from the TPN, so either possibility can be used with no adjustment. Choose the arrangement that looks better.

However, if:
Main stitch pattern repeat = 24 stitches.
TPN = 60 stitches.
Stockinette gauge = 8 st/in.
Then:
2 repeats of the main stitch pattern is 48 stitches. This is 12 stitches too few.

3 repeats of the main stitch pattern is 72 stitches. This is 12 stitches too many.

Either way, the number of stitches is too far outside of the acceptable range. We'll have to go back to the drawing board.

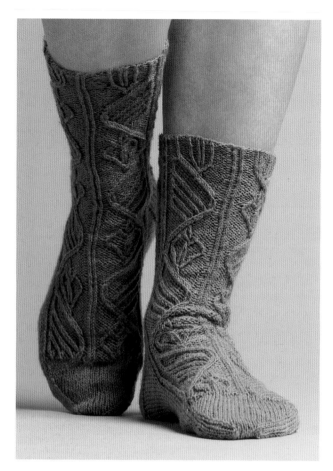

and smaller needles, 72 stitches could be knit densely enough to get the right size. Of course, if you use a much thicker yarn, the sock may not fit as comfortably inside a shoe.

Add additional vertical elements to widen the sock.
By adding extra vertical panels, a sock can be widened. In the example above, if a 12-stitch panel is added to the 48 stitches, the target 60 stitches will be reached. The additional stitches don't need to come from only one panel; they could come from two 6-stitch panels or a combination of a 6-stitch panel with two 3-stitch panels.

Modify the stitch pattern.
The most complicated solution is to modify the stitch pattern by widening or narrowing it until the APN is within the TPN range. In the above example, if 4 stitches can be removed from the stitch pattern, three repeats would give 60 stitches around—perfect. Alternatively, if 6 stitches could be added, two repeats would also give 60 stitches.

Of course, any modification to the main stitch pattern will affect the cuff. Re-calculate the ribbing and transition as necessary.

THE GAUGE SWATCH, TAKE TWO
Once you've decided on your cuff pattern, your main stitch pattern, the number of repeats, and how you will transition from the cuff to the main pattern, you're ready to cast on! Cast on the correct number for the cuff and join in the round. Remember, this number could be different from the APN if there are increases or decreases from the cuff to the main pattern. Work your cuff pattern for the desired length, transition to the main pattern on the leg, and work until the sock measures at least 3 inches or you've completed a full repeat of the pattern, whichever comes *last*. This will give you enough room to see the whole pattern and check the fit.

BACK TO THE DRAWING BOARD
Sometimes your chosen stitch pattern and your TPN won't work out quite right. In the last example, if the chosen stitch pattern is to be used, the sock will be too small or too big. We'll have to go back and change something. There are three main options:

Use thicker or thinner yarn and larger or smaller needles to alter the gauge.
This is the easiest way to change the size of a sock pattern, but it can change the look and feel of a pattern if a significantly different yarn is used. By using a thicker yarn and larger needles, 48 stitches might be large enough, where 60 stitches with fingering weight yarn was too small. Alternatively, by using thinner yarn

WHAT TO LOOK FOR IN
THE GAUGE SWATCH

After knitting a few inches beyond the cuff, it's time to examine the gauge swatch. Most importantly, check the fit. Don't just slide the swatch over your foot, try it on over the ankle as well as the leg. Can it slide over the ankle? How does it fit on the leg? If it's too small (**1**), stretch the fabric a reasonable amount and take a measurement. If it's too big (**2**), pinch the fabric and measure the excess. Use these measurements to calculate a new TPN and go back to the drawing board if necessary.

If the fit is right, how does it look? Are you happy with the tran-sition from the cuff to the main pattern? Do all the elements line up? How is the spacing between elements in the main pattern? If anything looks off, go back to the drawing board and make some changes.

How is the elasticity? If the fabric has too much drape, perhaps converting some areas to ribbing would be in order. Don't fool yourself into thinking the sock fits or looks okay if it doesn't. Three inches isn't much of an investment in the pattern. It's much better to rip out sooner rather than later.

If everything looks good, you're ready to continue with the rest of the sock.

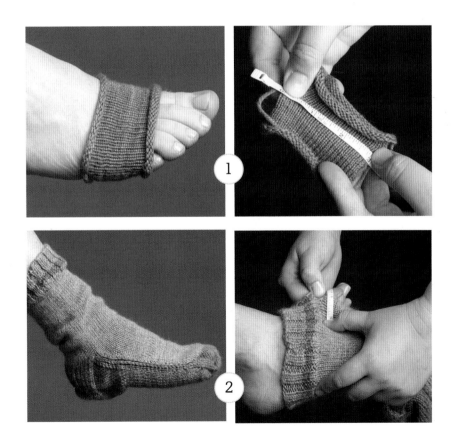

Planning Ahead to Put It All Together

Once you've gotten a decent way into the leg of the sock, you should begin to have a good feel for how the stitches are working and how the pattern is developing on the needles. It's time to think ahead to dividing for the heel flap and the top of the foot. If you want to use as much of your yarn as possible, your feet are wide or long, or you just don't have as much yarn as you think you'll need, calculations are needed to determine how long you can make the leg and where you can place the heel without running out of yarn before finishing the socks. (See page 55 for more information on yarn amount.)

DIVIDING FOR THE HEEL AND TOP OF FOOT

When to begin the divide, where to place it, and how to arrange the stitches on the needle are among the most important decisions in sock design. You'll need to consider both vertical and horizontal placement of the heel. While working on the leg of your sock, think about a good place to position the heel in the pattern to keep the flow of the design. By deciding where to place the heel, you are determining which stitches will flow into the top of the foot and which stitches will flow into the heel **1**.

Review The Art of Placement (page 21) for placement options and Converting Allover In-The-Round to Rectangular (page 37) to chart the rectangular top of foot section.

A long vertical pattern repeat can limit your leg length options if you want to end at a specific point in your pattern. If you realize that you won't be able to achieve the desired cuff length and line the elements up just so, consider starting over at a different place in the pattern.

In this example, the target length is 7" (18 cm), but one repeat gives a 5" (12.5 cm) leg and two repeats will measure 8" (20.5 cm) **2**. To achieve the target length, the top of the leg could be altered by removing the cuff ribbing. Alternatively, you could go back to the drawing board and shorten the pattern repeat length.

The division for the heel and top of the foot won't always fall neatly at the beginning of the round or between pattern repeats. You may want to add an extra stitch to one or both sides of the top of the foot for visual effect and symmetry. Similarly, you may want to add extra stitches to each side of the heel if you plan to continue in pattern on the heel, keeping in mind that the first stitch of each side of the heel will be slipped. Choose where to

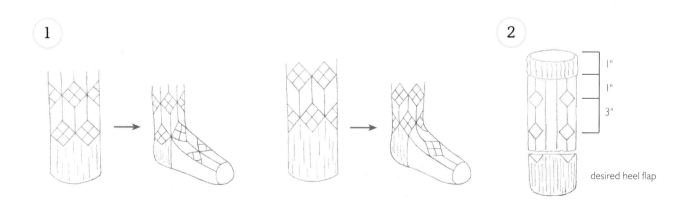

1

2

1"
1"
3"

desired heel flap

divide carefully—avoid placing the beginning of the round on the top of the foot, and if you plan to continue in pattern on a heel flap, avoid placing the beginning of the round on the heel flap. If the pattern staggers horizontally, line up the division such that the next repeat will be aligned to the right or left side of the sock.

TRANSITIONS

There are three major transitions to consider in your sock design: cuff to leg, leg to heel, and top of foot to toe. The cuff to leg transition was planned before you began knitting. If the heel will be in a different stitch pattern from the leg, such as slipped stitch or stockinette, you may need to decrease or increase stitches to avoid puckering if the pattern gauge is different from the stockinette gauge. Use cable decreases (see page 48) to transition from a cabled pattern to the heel if you do not plan to work the heel in pattern. Even if you continue in pattern onto a heel flap, since the heel turn is done in stockinette stitch, increasing or decreasing at the end of the heel flap may be necessary to match the stockinette gauge. Similarly, you may need to increase or decrease on the round immediately before the toe. Sometimes decreases or increases are better placed on certain rows within the pattern, so think ahead and plan accordingly. For examples of cable transitions, look at the cabled patterns in this book.

COORDINATING HEELS AND TOES

There is a wide variety of heels and toes to choose from; for some of the choices, see Heel Options (page 15) and Toe Options (page 20). Since these components are interchangeable, think ahead to what type of patterning you would like to use on your heels and toes. If you plan to continue in pattern on a heel flap, review Converting Allover In-The-Round to Rectangular (page 37) to chart the heel flap.

Toe placement is simpler than heel placement. After increasing or decreasing as necessary for the transition from pattern to the toe, count the number of stitches on the top of the foot and the number of stitches in the sole (the remaining stitches). If there are more stitches on the top or bottom, move one stitch from each edge to the other side until the top and the bottom both have the same number of stitches. This will maintain the centering of the pattern on top of the foot and make sure that the toe is properly positioned. If the number cannot be divided evenly, decrease as necessary to make the stitch count even.

YARN AMOUNT

It's difficult to provide accurate yarn amount estimates because people knit so differently and row gauges can vary wildly even when stitch gauges are the same. I recommend beginning with extra yarn just in case. Especially when designing, it is better to have too much rather than too little.

To double-check your yarn usage, you can do weight comparisons. By weighing the amount of yarn you've already knitted and comparing that with how much you have left to knit and how much yarn remains, you can do an eyeball comparison. For example, if you've already worked through half the yarn you have for one sock, but you haven't reached the heel yet, you probably won't have enough to complete the sock. Estimate what percentage of the sock is finished and what percentage of yarn has been used so far. Be honest! Maybe you can put another ball of yarn on hold at your local yarn store until you know whether you'll need it or not.

If there's a chance you won't have enough yarn, it's better to know earlier because it gives you more options. Here are some yarn-saving tips:

- Use an afterthought heel. After the rest of the socks are completed, see how much yarn you have left over. If it's not enough to complete the heels, substitute a contrasting yarn.
- Work a short-row heel instead of a heel flap and gusset. A short-row heel uses less yarn, but it may not fit as well if you have a high instep.
- Transition to stockinette for the top of the foot. Stockinette stitch uses less yarn than heavily textured patterns.
- Shorten the cuff or leg of the sock.
- Work the toes with a different yarn.

socks to knit

Using these techniques, I created the following fifteen sock patterns. By keeping the techniques in mind as you knit these, you'll begin to get a feel for transitions, placement, and the connection between charts and the knitted fabric. If you feel a little bit adventurous, modify these patterns to fit your needs. Once you are comfortable with customizing existing sock patterns, branch out on your own. There are many stitch pattern books to peruse for ideas and inspiration. Or, if you are a truly adventurous knitter, try devising your own! There are so many possibilities, and the sock can be your empty canvas.

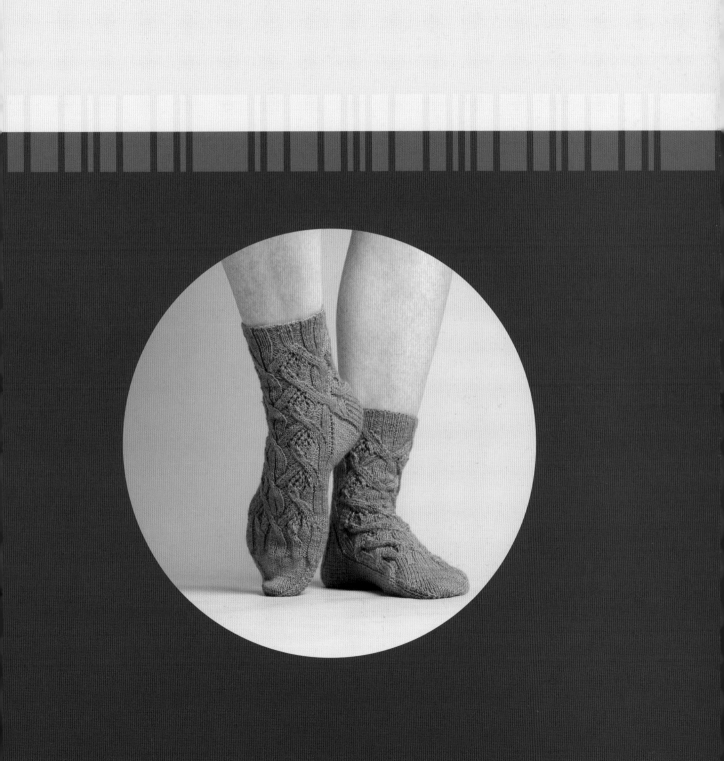

glynis

The first time I met my mother-in-law, Glynis, we went for a drive in the mountains along the coast. I could see the fear in her green eyes every time we turned a corner. These socks are perfect for trepid knitters interested in lace, because they are much simpler than they appear. Like Devon (see page 72) they have an intentional asymmetry between the right and left socks, but these have a relaxing plain round between pattern rounds.

Finished Measurements
Leg circumference—8" (20.5 cm), slightly stretched.
Foot circumference—8¼" (21 cm), slightly stretched.

Yarn
Fingering weight (Super Fine #1).
Shown here: Shibui Knits (100% superwash Merino wool; 191 yd [175 m]/50 g): Wasabi, 2 skeins.

Needles
U.S. size 1½ (2.5 mm): circular (cir) or double-pointed (dpn). Adjust needle size if necessary to obtain the correct gauge.

Notions
Markers (m; optional); tapestry needle.

Gauge
30 stitches and 46 rounds = 4" (10 cm) in stockinette stitch in the round.
30 stitches and about 43 rounds = 4" (10 cm) in pattern stitch in the round, slightly stretched.

Sizing
The overall pattern is made with such short lines that the best way to resize would be to change gauge with thinner or thicker yarn and appropriate needles or to add or remove repeats.

Knitting Chart Symbols

□ Knit
• Purl
○ Yarnover
⊠ Ssk
⊡ K2tog
⊠ Sssk
⊠ K3tog
⊻ Kfbf
■ No stitch
□ Pattern repeat

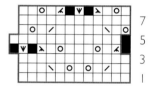

Ribbing
(multiple of 12 sts; 1 rnd rep)

•	•		•	•		•	•		•		1

Set-up
(multiple of 12 sts; 3 rnds)

	○	⊠	⊻	■	⊠		○		3
○	⊡	•	•		•	•	⊠	○	1

Leg
(multiple of 12 sts; 8 rnd rep)

	○	⊠	⊻	■	⊠		○		7
○	⊡					⊠	○		5
⊻	⊠		○			○		⊠	3
		⊠	○	○	⊡				1

Note: On Rnd 5 of Leg chart, do not work last st in rnd. Move marker indicating beg of rnd 1 st to the right.

Cuff
RIBBING

CO 60 sts. Being careful not to twist sts, join for working in the round and place marker (pm) for beg of rnd.

Work Ribbing chart for 1" (2.5 cm).

SET UP FOR LEG

Work Rnds 1–3 from Set-up chart.

Leg

Work Leg chart across all sts 9 times, ending after Rnd 8.

Heel

HEEL FLAP

Divide for heel flap as foll: Place previous 31 sts on hold for top of foot; rem 29 sts will be worked back and forth for heel flap.

ROW 1: (RS) [Sl 1 purlwise (pwise) with yarn in back (wyb), k1] 14 times, k1, turn.

ROW 2: Sl 1 pwise with yarn in front (wyf), p28, turn.

Rep Rows 1 and 2 until heel flap measures 2¼–2½" (5.5–6.5 cm) or desired length, ending after Row 2.

TURN HEEL

Work back and forth in short-rows to shape heel.

SHORT-ROW 1: (RS) Sl 1 pwise wyb, k15, ssk, k1, turn.

SHORT-ROW 2: Sl 1 pwise wyf, p4, p2tog, p1, turn.

SHORT-ROW 3: Sl 1, knit to 1 st before gap created on previous row, ssk (1 st from each side of gap), k1, turn.

SHORT-ROW 4: Sl 1, purl to 1 st before gap created on previous row, p2tog (1 st from each side of gap), p1, turn.

Rep Short-rows 3 and 4 until all sts have been worked—17 heel sts rem.

SHAPE GUSSETS

Note: Where possible, arrange sts so that marker placement occurs between needles.

SET-UP RND: Sl 1 pwise wyb, k7, pm for beg of rnd, k9, pick up and knit (see Glossary) 1 st in each sl st along edge of heel flap plus 1 st between heel flap and top of foot, pm for right side of foot, resume working in the rnd on held sts by working Rnd 1 from Top of Foot chart, pm for left side of foot; pick up and knit 1 st between top of foot and heel flap and 1 st in each sl st along edge of heel flap, k8.

RND 1: Knit to 2 sts before right m, k2tog, work next rnd from Top of Foot chart, ssk, knit to end—2 sts dec'd.

RND 2: Knit to right m, work next rnd from Top of Foot chart, knit to end.

Rep Rnds 1 and 2 until 62 sts rem (31 sts each for top of foot and sole).

Top of Foot
(panel of 31 sts; 8 rnd rep)

Foot

Work even in patt until foot measures 2" (5 cm) less than desired length from back of heel. Remove m for beg of rnd and knit to right m (new beg of rnd).

Toe

RND 1: Knit.

RND 2: K1, ssk, knit to 3 sts before left side m, k2tog, k1, k1, ssk, knit to 3 sts before right m, k2tog, k1—4 sts dec'd.

Rep Rnds 1 and 2 ten more times—18 sts rem. Divide sts evenly over 2 needles so that there are 9 sts each for top of foot and sole. Cut yarn, leaving a 12" (30.5 cm) tail. With tail threaded on tapestry needle, use the Kitchener st (see Glossary) to graft sts. Weave in ends.

$\mathcal{E}$ unice and I like to joke that we are the same person. We have very different interests—Eunice barely knits—but deep down we think an awful lot alike. These are very much what I like in socks, so I know Eunice would love these if she were a hardcore sock knitter. These have cables, lace, jogs, and an interesting pattern to transition to the slipped-stitch heel. The cuff is short, also perfect for petite Eunice.

Finished Measurements

Leg circumference—8" (20.5 cm), slightly stretched.
Foot circumference—8" (20.5 cm), slightly stretched.

Yarn

Fingering weight (Super Fine #1).
Shown here: Koigu Premium Merino (100% wool; 175 yd [160 m]/50 g): #1500 teal, 2 skeins.

Needles

U.S. size 1 (2.25 mm): circular (cir) or double-pointed (dpn). Adjust needle size of necessary to obtain the correct gauge.

Notions

Two cable needles (cn); markers (m; optional); tapestry needle.

Gauge

32 stitches and 47 rounds = 4" (10 cm) in stockinette stitch in the round.
40 stitches and 47 rounds = 4" (10 cm) in pattern in the round, slightly stretched.

Sizing

See pages 46–47.

stitch guide

Cross 3L

Sl 3 sts onto cn and hold in front, sl 1 st onto second cn and hold in back, k3, p1 from second cn, k3 from first cn.

Cross 3L Dec1

Sl 3 sts onto cn and hold in front, k2tog, k2, k3 from cn—1 st dec'd.

Cross 3L Dec4

Sl 3 sts onto cn and hold in front, knit first st from cn tog with 2 sts from left needle, [knit next st from cn tog with 1 st from left needle] two times—4 sts dec'd.

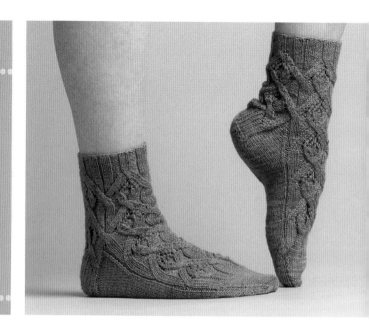

Ribbing
(multiple of 16 sts; 1 rnd rep)

- □ Knit on RS; purl on WS
- ● Purl on RS; knit on WS
- Knit into front, back, front, back, front of same st
- ⋁ Slip st purlwise wyb on RS, wyf on WS
- ○ Yarnover
- ⟋ K2tog
- ⟍ Ssk
- P Make 1 purlwise
- These 4 sts are included in the pattern rep, BUT omit these 4 sts from the last rep and end rnd 4 sts early.
- These 4 sts are NOT included in the pattern rep. Work these 4 sts at the end of rnd only.
- Cross 3L
- Cross 3L Dec 1
- Cross 3L Dec 4
- ■ No stitch
- □ Pattern repeat

Set-up
(multiple of 16 sts inc'd to multiple of 20 sts; 1 rnd rep)

Leg
(multiple of 20 sts; 20 rnd rep)

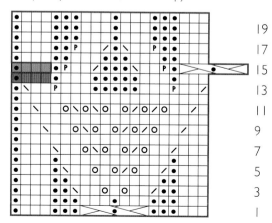

Cuff

RIBBING

CO 64 sts. Being careful not to twist sts, join for working in the round and place marker (pm) for beg of rnd.

 Work Ribbing chart for 1" (2.5 cm).

SET UP FOR LEG

Work Set-up chart—80 sts.

Leg

Work Leg chart 2 times.

Note: On Rnd 14, beg of rnd shifts 4 sts to the right; work Rnd 14 from chart 3 times, then work first 16 stitches of rnd again, omitting last 4 sts. Pm to indicate new beg of rnd. On Rnd 15, shift beg of rnd 4 sts to the left (back to its original position): working Rnd 15 of chart 4 times, remove m, work blue sts from chart, pm. Work Rnds 16–20 as shown.

Heel

HEEL FLAP

Divide for Heel Flap as foll: Place previous 41 sts on hold for top of foot; rem 39 sts will be worked back and forth for heel flap.

 Work Rows 1–18 of Heel chart, then rep Rows 17–18 until heel flap measures 2¼–2½" (5.5–6.5 cm) or desired length, ending after Row 18—31 sts.

TURN HEEL

Work back and forth in short-rows to shape heel.

SHORT-ROW 1: (RS) Sl 1 purlwise (pwise) with yarn in back (wyb), k17, ssk, k1, turn.

SHORT-ROW 2: (WS) Sl 1 pwise with yarn in front (wyf), p6, p2tog, p1, turn.

SHORT-ROW 3: Sl 1 pwise wyb, knit to 1 st before gap created on previous row, ssk (1 st from each side of gap), k1, turn.

SHORT-ROW 4: Sl 1 pwise wyf, purl to 1 st before gap created on previous row, p2tog (1 st from each side of gap), p1, turn.

Rep Short-rows 3 and 4 until all stitches have been worked—19 heel sts rem.

Heel
(panel of 39 sts dec'd to 31 sts; 18 rows)

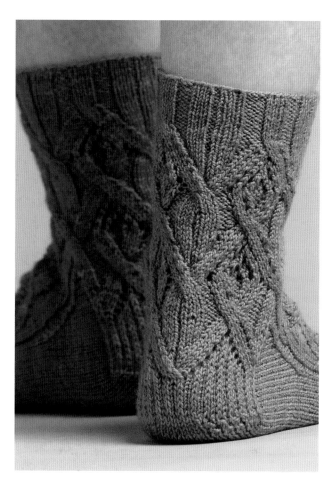

SHAPE GUSSETS

Note: Where possible, arrange sts so that marker placement occurs between needles.

SET-UP RND: Sl 1 pwise wyb, k8, pm for beg of rnd, k10, pick up and knit (see Glossary) 1 st in each sl st along edge of heel flap plus 1 st between heel flap and top of foot, pm for right side of foot, resume working in the rnd on held sts by working Rnd 1 from Top of Foot chart; pm to indicate left side of foot; pick up and knit 1 st between top of foot and heel flap and 1 st in each sl st along other edge of heel flap, k9.

RND 1: Knit to 2 sts before right m, k2tog, work next rnd from Top of Foot chart, ssk, knit to end—2 sts dec'd.

RND 2: Knit to right m, work next rnd from Top of Foot chart, knit to end.

Rep Rnds 1 and 2 until 74 sts rem (41 sts for top of foot and 33 sts for sole).

Top of Foot
(panel of 41 sts; 20 rnd rep)

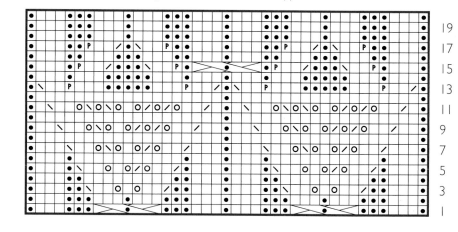

Decrease Version 1
(panel of 41 sts dec'd to 33 sts; 2 rnds)

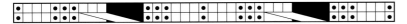

Decrease Version 2
(panel of 41 sts dec'd to 33 sts; 4 rnds)

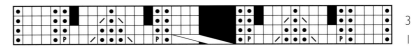

3

1

Foot

Work even in patt (working 41 top of foot sts following chart and 33 sole sts in St st) until foot measures 4" (10 cm) less than desired length from back of heel, noting last rnd worked and keeping m in place.

Dec 8 sts over next 2" (5 cm) as foll:

- If last rnd worked was between Rnds 6 and 16 of Top of Foot chart, continue in patt through Rnd 20 of chart, then work Decrease Version 1 chart over top of foot sts after completing Rnd 20—33 sts rem for top of foot; 66 sts total.
- If last rnd worked was between Rnds 1 and 5 or 17 and 20, continue in patt to end of Rnd 14 of Top of Foot chart, then work Decrease Version 2 chart over top of foot sts after completing Rnd 14—33 sts rem for top of foot; 66 sts total.

For both versions, rep last rnd (following last row of Decrease chart) until foot measures 2" (5 cm) less than desired length from back of heel.

Toe

Remove m for beg of rnd, knit to right m (new beg of rnd).

RND 1: Knit.

RND 2: K1, ssk, knit to 3 sts before left m, k2tog, k1, k1, ssk, knit to 3 sts before m indicating right side of foot, k2tog, k1—4 sts dec'd.

Rep Rnds 1 and 2 eleven more times—18 sts rem. Divide sts evenly over 2 needles so that there are 9 sts each for top of foot and sole.

Finish

Cut yarn, leaving a 12" (30.5 cm) tail. With tail threaded on a tapestry needle, use the Kitchener st (see Glossary) to graft sts. Weave in ends.

sunshine

*T*hese peachy socks are named after a little bundle of joy (four months as of this writing) named Sunshine. They are straightforward, just like she is, with simple vertical repeats. A smattering of cables and lace make these socks a little bit interesting without too much strain. I hope Sunny T, as I like to call her, grows up to be a knitter unlike her mother, Eunice. Even if she doesn't, she'll still be loved.

Finished Measurements
Leg circumference—8" (20.5 cm), slightly stretched.
Foot circumference—8" (20.5 cm), slightly stretched.

Yarn
Fingering weight (Super Fine #1).
Shown here: Artyarns Ultramerino 4 (100% wool; 191 yd [175 m]/50 g): #221, 2 skeins.

Needles
U.S. size 1½ (2.5 mm): circular (cir) or double-pointed (dpn). Adjust needle size if necessary to obtain the correct gauge.

Notions
Cable needle (cn); markers (m; optional); tapestry needle.

Gauge
30 stitches and 45 rounds = 4" (10 cm) in stockinette stitch in the round.
40 stitches and 47 rounds = 4" (10 cm) in lace/cable pattern in the round, slightly stretched.

Sizing
To resize, add or remove repeats.

stitch guide

Cable 2K L 2K
Sl 2 sts to cn and hold in front of work, k2 from left needle, k2 from cn.

Cable 2K R 2K
Sl 2 sts to cn and hold in back of work, k2 from left needle, k2 from cn.

Cable Decrease 2 Left
Sl 2 sts to cn and hold in front of work, [knit 1 st from cn tog with 1 st from left needle] 2 times—2 sts dec'd.

Cable Decrease 2 Right
Sl 2 sts to cn and hold in back of work, [knit 1 st from left needle tog with 1 st from cn] 2 times—2 sts dec'd.

Ribbing
(multiple of 6 sts; 1 rnd rep)

Set-up
(multiple of 6 sts inc'd to 8 sts sts; 2 rnds)

□ Knit
• Purl
Ⅴ Kfbf
■ No stitch
◙ Yarnover
◪ Ssk
☑ K2tog
⬚ Cable 2K L 2K
⬚ Cable 2K R 2K
□ Pattern repeat

Leg
(multiple of 8 sts; 20 rnd rep)

Cuff
RIBBING

CO 60. Being careful not to twist stitches, join for working in the round and place marker (pm) for beg of rnd.
Work Ribbing chart for 1" (2.5 cm).

SET UP FOR LEG
Work Rnds 1 and 2 of Set-up chart—80 sts.

Leg

Work Rnds 1–20 of Leg chart across all sts 2 times, then work Rnds 1–19 of Leg chart once more (59 rnds total).

NEXT RND: Work Rnd 20 over 40 sts (5 times), [k2, Cable Decrease 2 Right, p2] 4 times, k2, Cable Decrease 2 Right; *do not* work last 2 sts of rnd—70 sts rem.

Heel
HEEL FLAP
Divide for heel flap as foll: Place 2 unworked sts from last rnd and next 40 sts on hold for top of foot; rem 28 sts will be worked back and forth for heel flap. Turn work.

ROW 1: (WS) Sl 1 purlwise (pwise) with yarn in front (wyf), p27, turn.

ROW 2: [Sl 1 pwise with yarn in back (wyb), k1] 14 times, turn.

Rep Rows 1 and 2 until heel flap measures 2¼–2½" (5.5–6.5 cm) or desired length, ending after Row 1.

TURN HEEL
Work back and forth in short-rows to shape heel.

SHORT-ROW 1: (RS) Sl 1 pwise wyb, k16, ssk, k1, turn.

SHORT-ROW 2: Sl 1 pwise wyf, p7, p2tog, p1, turn.

SHORT-ROW 3: Sl 1 pwise wyb, knit to 1 st before gap created on previous row, ssk (1 st from each side of gap), k1, turn.

SHORT-ROW 4: Sl 1 pwise wyf, purl to 1 st before gap created on previous row, p2tog (1 st from each side of gap), p1, turn.

Rep Short-rows 3 and 4 until all sts have been worked—18 heel sts rem.

SHAPE GUSSETS
Note: Where possible, arrange sts so that marker placement occurs between needles.

SET-UP RND: Sl 1 pwise wyb, k8, pm for beginning of round, k9, pick up and knit (see Glossary) 1 st in each sl st along edge of heel flap plus 1 st between heel flap and top of foot, pm for foot right side, resume working in the rnd on held sts by working Rnd 1 from Top of Foot chart, pm for foot left side, pick up and knit 1 st between top of foot and heel flap and 1 st in each sl st along edge of heel flap, k9.

RND 1: Knit to 2 sts before right m, k2tog, work in patt (following Top of Foot chart) to left m, ssk, knit to beginning of rnd m—2 sts dec'd.

RND 2: Knit to right m, work in patt to left m, sl m, knit to beginning of rnd m.

Rep Rnds 1 and 2 until 70 sts rem (42 sts for top of foot and 28 sts for sole).

Top of Foot
(multiple of 8 sts + 2;
20 rnd rep)

Foot
Work even in patt until foot measures about (but not more than) 2" (5 cm) less than desired length from back of heel, ending with Rnd 9 or 19 of Top of Foot chart. Dec 10 sts on next rnd as foll:

- If last rnd worked was Row 9, knit to right m, [p2, Cable Decrease 2 Left, k2] 5 times, p2—60 sts rem (32 sts for top of foot, 28 sts for sole).
- If last rnd worked was Rnd 19, knit to right m, [p2, k2, Cable Decrease 2 Right] 5 times, p2—60 sts rem (32 sts for top of foot, 28 sts for sole).

Sl first and last sts from top of foot to sole—30 sts each for top of foot and sole.

Work even in St st until foot measures 2" (5 cm) less than desired length from back of heel. Remove m for beginning of round, knit to right m (new beg of rnd).

Toe
RND 1: Knit.

RND 2: K1, ssk, knit to 3 sts before left m, k2tog, k1, k1, ssk, knit to 3 sts before m, k2tog, k1—4 sts dec'd.

Rep Rnds 1 and 2 ten more times—16 sts rem. Divide sts evenly over 2 needles so that there are 8 sts each for top of foot and sole.

Finishing
Cut yarn, leaving a 12" (30.5 cm) tail. With tail threaded on a tapestry needle, use the Kitchener st (see Glossary) to graft sts. Weave in ends.

devon

y sister-in-law is a teenager and probably isn't sure what she wants to be when she grows up. These playful socks aren't sure if they'd rather be solid or multicolored. The stitches are divided asymmetrically for the heel and instep so that one repeat on one side is cut in half. While the left and right socks aren't mirrored to preserve the asymmetry, it wouldn't be difficult to create a mirrored chart.

Finished Measurements

Leg circumference—8" (20.5 cm), slightly stretched.
Foot circumference—8¼" (20.5 cm), slightly stretched.

Yarn

Fingering weight (Super Fine #1).
Shown here: Solid version—Mountain Colors Bearfoot (60% superwash wool, 25% mohair, 15% nylon; 350 yd [320 m]/100 g): magenta, 1 skein. Variegated version—Claudia Hand Painted Yarn Fingering (100% wool; 175 yd [160 m]/50 g): John B, 2 skeins.

Needles

U.S. size 1½ (2.5 mm): circular (cir) or double-pointed (dpn). Adjust needle size if necessary to obtain the correct gauge.

Notions

Markers (m; optional); tapestry needle.

Gauge

30 stitches and 41 rounds = 4" (10 cm) in stockinette stitch in the round.
30 stitches and 38 rounds = 4" (10 cm) in pattern in the round, slightly stretched.

Sizing

To resize this sock, I recommend enlarging or reducing the stitch pattern by decreasing the number of stitches and rows in the inner diamonds (see pages 46–47).

stitch guide

Double decrease

On RS: Sl 1 knitwise (kwise) with yarn in back
(wyb), k2tog, psso.

On WS: P2tog, sl 1 kwise with yarn in front
(wyf), pass 2 sts purlwise (pwise) from right
needle to left needle, pass second st on left
needle over first st, sl 1 pwise wyf.

- ☐ Knit on RS; purl on WS
- ⊡ Purl on RS; knit on WS
- ⊙ Yarnover
- ◩ Ssk on RS; ssp on WS
- ☑ K2tog on RS; p2tog on WS
- ◮ Double decrease
- ◮ Double decrease EXCEPT at beg of rnd — k2tog,
  pass last st from previous rnd over new st
- ☑ Slip stitch purlwise wyb on RS, wyf on WS
- ☐ Pattern repeat

Cuff
RIBBING
CO 60 sts. Being careful not to twist stitches, join for working in
the round and place marker (pm) for beg of rnd.
  Work Ribbing chart for 1" (5 cm).

SET UP FOR LEG
Work Rnds 1–5 of Set-up chart.

Leg
Work all sts following Leg chart 4 times.
Note: On Rnds 5 and 9 of Leg chart, the first double decrease
in the round is worked using the first 2 sts of the round together
with the last st from the previous round. Knit the first 2 sts after
m together and pass 2nd st on right needle (last st from previous
round) over newly formed st. Replace marker before this st.

Heel
HEEL FLAP
Divide for heel flap as foll: Place next 31 sts on hold for top of
foot; rem 29 sts will be worked back and forth for heel flap.
  Turn work so that WS is facing. Work Rows 1–9 of Heel chart,
beginning with Row 1 on WS (working from left to right). Rep
Rows 8–9 until heel flap measures 2¼–2½" (5.5–6.5 cm) or
desired length, ending after Row 9.

Ribbing
(multiple of 12 sts; 1 rnd rep)

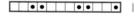

Set-up
(multiple of 12 sts; 5 rnds)

Leg
(multiple of 12 sts; 18 rnd rep)

17
15
13
11
9
7
5
3
1

Heel
(panel of 29 sts; 9 rows)

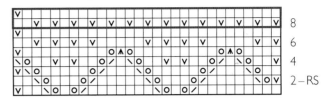

8
6
4
2 – RS

TURN HEEL

Work back and forth in short-rows to shape heel.

SHORT-ROW 1: (RS) Sl 1 pwise wyb, k15, ssk, k1, turn.

SHORT-ROW 2: Sl 1 pwise wyf, p4, p2tog, p1, turn.

SHORT-ROW 3: Sl 1 pwise wyb, knit to 1 st before gap created on previous row, ssk (1 st from each side of gap), k1, turn.

SHORT-ROW 4: Sl 1 pwise wyf, purl to 1 st before gap created on previous row, p2tog (1 st from each side of gap), p1, turn.

Rep Short-rows 3 and 4 until all sts have been worked—17 heel sts rem.

SHAPE GUSSETS

Note: Where possible, arrange sts so that marker placement occurs between needles.

SET-UP RND: Sl 1 pwise wyb, k7, pm for beg of round, k9, pick up and knit (see Glossary) 1 st in each sl st along edge of heel flap plus 1 st between heel flap and top of foot, pm for right side of foot, resume working in the rnd on held sts by working Rnd 1 of Top of Foot chart, pm for left side of foot, pick up and knit 1 st between top of foot and heel flap and 1 st in each sl st along edge of heel flap, k8.

RND 1: Knit to 2 sts before right m, k2tog, work in patt as established (following Top of Foot chart), ssk, knit to end—2 sts dec'd.

RND 2: Knit to right m, work in patt as established to left m, knit to marker indicating beginning of rnd.

Rep Rnds 1 and 2 until 62 sts rem on needles (31 sts each for top of foot and sole).

Foot

Work even in patt until foot measures 2" (5 cm) less than desired length from back of heel.

Toe

Remove m for beginning of round, knit to right m (new beg of rnd).

RND 1: Knit.

RND 2: K1, ssk, knit to 3 sts before left m, k2tog, k1, sl m, k1, ssk, knit to 3 sts before right m, k2tog, k1—4 sts dec'd.

Rep Rnds 1 and 2 ten more times—18 sts rem. Divide sts evenly over 2 needles so that there are 9 sts each for top of foot and sole.

Finish

Cut yarn, leaving a 12" (30 cm) tail. With tail threaded on a tapestry needle, use the Kitchener stitch (see Glossary) to graft sts. Weave in ends.

Top of Foot
(panel of 31 sts; 18 rnd rep)

17
15
13
11
9
7
5
3
1

vilai

*T*hese socks, inspired by a stitch pattern from a Japanese book, are named after my mother. One of my favorite photos of her is an old black-and-white where she posed in a kimono. Apparently we both have a fascination with the Japanese. This stitch pattern was fun to play with, and I experimented with different backgrounds and widths before settling on one.

Finished Measurements

Leg circumference—8" (20.5 cm), slightly stretched.
Foot circumference—8½" (21.5 cm), slightly stretched.

Yarn

Fingering weight (Super Fine #1).
Shown here: Solid version—Lorna's Laces Shepherd Sock (80% superwash wool, 20% nylon; 215 yd [197 m]/2 oz): Cranberry, 2 skeins. Variegated version (page 79)—Blue Moon Fiber Arts Socks That Rock Lightweight (100% superwash Merino; 360 yd [329 m]/4.5 oz): Purple Rain, 1 skein.

Needles

U.S. size 1 (2.25 mm): circular (cir) or double-pointed (dpn). Adjust needle size if necessary to obtain the correct gauge.

Notions

2 cable needles (cn); markers (m; optional); tapestry needle.

Gauge

32 stitches and 48 rounds = 4" (10 cm) in stockinette stitch in the round.
36 stitches and 50 rounds = 4" (10 cm) in pattern in the round, slightly stretched.

Sizing

While it's possible to resize the pattern by narrowing or widening the rib and lace areas, the easiest method is to use thicker or thinner yarn and needles.

stitch guide

Rib Cross 3L

Sl 3 sts to cn and hold in front, sl 1 st to second cn and hold in back, k1 tbl, p1, k1 tbl; p1 from second cn; k1 tbl, p1, k1tbl from first cn.

Rib Cross 3L Dec4

Sl 3 sts to cn and hold in front, knit first st from cn together with 2 stitches from left needle through back loops (2 sts dec'd), purl 1 st stitch from cn together with 1 st from left needle (1 st dec'd), knit rem st from cn together with next st from left needle through back loops (1 st dec'd)—4 st dec'd total.

℞ Knit tbl		 Rib Cross 3L	
☐ Knit		 Rib Cross 3L Dec4	
• Purl		Ⓥ Kfbfbf	
⊙ Yarnover		☐ Pattern repeat	
⃮ K2tog		■ No stitch	
⃰ Ssk			
⃰ K3tog			
⃰ Sssk			

Ribbing
(multiple of 32 sts; 1 rnd rep)

Set-up
(multiple of 32 sts inc'd to 36 sts; 2 rnds)

Pattern
(panel of 35 sts; 28 rnd rep)

27
25
23
21
19
17
15
13
11
9
7
5
3
1

Cuff

RIBBING

CO 64 sts. Being careful not to twist stitches, join for working in the round and place marker (pm) for beg of rnd.

Work Ribbing chart for 1" (2.5 cm).

SET UP FOR LEG

Work Rnds 1 and 2 of Set-up chart—72 sts.

Leg

RNDS 1–28: *K1, work Pattern chart; rep from * to end of rnd. Rep Rnds 1–28 once more, then rep Rnds 1–13.

NEXT RND: K1, work Rnd 14 of Pattern chart over 35 sts, k1, work Dec Rnd 14 chart (page 80) to end of rnd—68 sts rem.

Heel

Note: The variegated version (pictured below) uses a short-row heel. See page 16 for instructions.

HEEL FLAP

Divide for heel flap as foll: Place next 37 sts on hold for top of foot; rem 31 sts will be worked back and forth for heel flap. Turn work so that WS is facing.

ROW 1: (WS) Sl 1 purlwise (pwise) with yarn in front (wyf), p30, turn.

ROW 2: [Sl 1 knitwise (kwise) with yarn in back (wyb), k1] 15 times, k1, turn.

Rep Rows 1 and 2 until heel flap measures 2¼–2½" (5.5–6.5 cm) or desired length, ending after Row 1.

Dec Rnd 14

(panel of 35 sts dec'd to 31 sts; 1 rnd)

Dec Rnd 28

(panel of 35 sts dec'd to 31 sts; 1 rnd)

TURN HEEL

Work back and forth in short-rows to shape heel.

SHORT-ROW 1: (RS) Sl 1 pwise wyb, k17, ssk, k1, turn.

SHORT-ROW 2: Sl 1 pwise wyf, p6, p2tog, p1, turn.

SHORT-ROW 3: Sl 1 pwise wyb, knit to 1 st before gap created on previous row, ssk (1 st from each side of gap), k1, turn.

SHORT-ROW 4: Sl 1 pwise wyf, purl to 1 st before gap created on previous row, p2tog (1 st from each side of gap), p1, turn.

Rep Short-rows 3 and 4 until all sts have been worked—19 heel sts rem.

SHAPE GUSSETS

Note: Where possible, arrange sts so that marker placement occurs between needles.

SET-UP RND: Sl 1 pwise wyb, k8, pm for beginning of round, k10, pick up and knit (see Glossary)1 st in each sl st along edge of heel flap plus 1 st between heel flap and top of foot. Resume working in the rnd over held sts as foll: k1, pm for right side of foot, work Rnd 15 of Pattern chart, pm for left side of foot, k1. Pick up and knit 1 st between top of foot and heel flap and 1 st in each sl st along edge of heel flap, k9.

RND 1: Knit to 2 st before right m, k2tog, work in patt as established to left m, ssk, knit to end—2 sts dec'd.

RND 2: Knit to right m, work in patt as established to left m, knit to end.

Rep Rnds 1 and 2 until 66 sts rem (35 sts for top of foot and 31 sts for sole).

Foot

Work even in patt until foot measures 2½" (6.5 cm) inches less than desired length from back of heel, ending on an even-numbered row. Dec 4 sts as foll:

- If last rnd worked was 8, 10, or 12, work in patt through Rnd 13 of chart. Work Dec Rnd 14 chart—62 sts rem.
- If last rnd worked was 22, 24, or 28, work in pattern through Rnd 27 of chart. Work Dec Rnd 28 chart—62 sts rem.
- If last rnd worked was any other rnd:

NEXT RND: Work in patt.

NEXT RND: Work sole sts in St st and work next rnd of chart *except* omit the first and last yos of chart.

NEXT RND: Work sole sts in St st and work next rnd of chart *except* omit the first and last sts of chart.

NEXT RND: Work sole sts in St st and work next rnd of pattern chart *except:*

- If chart begins with [yo, ssk, yo], replace sts in brackets with k1 and replace [yo, k2tog, yo] with k1 at end of chart.
- If chart begins with [k1, yo], omit those 2 sts and omit [yo, k1] at end.

NEXT RND: Work sole sts in St st and work next rnd of chart *except* omit 2 knit sts each from beg and end of chart section.

62 sts rem (31 sts each for top of foot and sole). If necessary, work in St st until foot measures 2" (5 cm) less than desired length from back of heel.

Toe

Remove m for beginning of round, knit to right m (new beg of rnd).

RND 1: Knit.

RND 2: K1, ssk, knit to 3 sts before left m, k2tog, k1, sl m, k1, ssk, knit to 3 sts before right m, k2tog, k1—4 sts dec'd.

Rep Rnds 1 and 2 ten more times—18 sts rem. Divide sts evenly over 2 needles so that there are 9 sts each for top of foot and sole.

Finish

Cut yarn, leaving a 12" (30 cm) tail. With tail threaded on a tapestry needle, use the Kitchener st (see Glossary) to graft sts. Weave in ends.

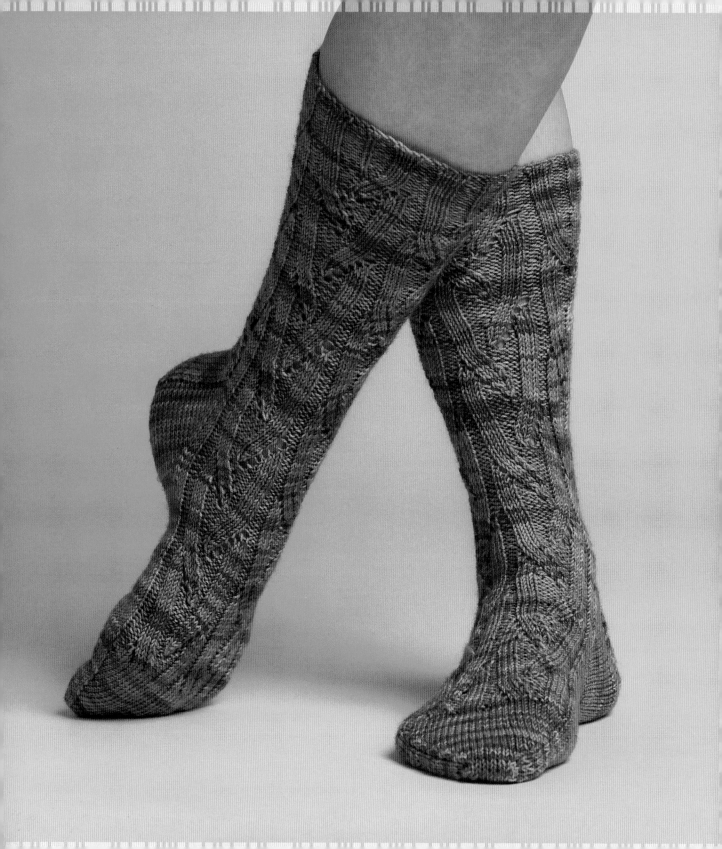

angee

y friend Angee is super cool, and in a lot of ways I'm just a wannabe Angee. She may very well be the start of my fascination with crazy colorful socks. Her collection (admittedly machine-knitted, not handknitted) contains polka dots, funky stripes, and all sorts of other wacky socks. These wonderfully bright orange socks feature an interesting textured pattern. They are straightforward and tell it like it is, just like Angee.

Finished Measurements

Leg circumference—8" (20.5 cm), slightly stretched.
Foot circumference—8" (20.5 cm), slightly stretched.

Yarn

Fingering weight (Super Fine #1).
Shown here: Colinette Jitterbug (100% Merino wool; 289 yd [264 m]/100 g): Ginger Cinnabar, 2 skeins.
Note: Pair can be made using 1 skein by removing one chart repeat from leg.

Needles

U.S. size 1½ (2.5 mm): circular (cir) or double-pointed (dpn). Adjust needle size if necessary to obtain the correct gauge.

Notions

Markers (m; optional); tapestry needle.

Gauge

32 stitches and 44 rounds = 4" (10 cm) stockinette stitch in the round.
32 stitches and 47 rounds = 4" (10 cm) inches in pattern in the round, slightly stretched.

Sizing

To resize these socks, add or remove columns of purl stitches from existing vertical purl lines.

Knit
- □ Knit
- ● Purl
- ⊙ Yarnover
- ╱ K2tog
- ╲ Ssk
- □ Pattern repeat

Ribbing
(multiple of 13 sts; 1 rnd rep)

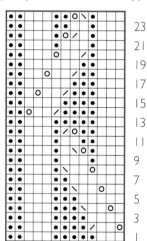

Set-up
(multiple of 13 sts; 12 rnds)

11
9
7
5
3

Leg
(multiple of 13 sts; 24 rnd rep)

23
21
19
17
15
13
11
9
7
5
3
1

Top of Foot
(panel of 32 sts; 24 rnd rep)

23
21
19
17
15
13
11
9
7
5
3
1

Cuff
RIBBING
CO 65 sts. Being careful not to twist stitches, join for working in the round and place marker (pm) for beginning of round.
   Work Ribbing chart for 1" (2.5 cm).

SET UP FOR LEG
Work Rnds 1–12 of Set-up chart.

Leg
Work Rnds 1–24 of Leg chart 2 times, then work Rnds 1–13 one more time.

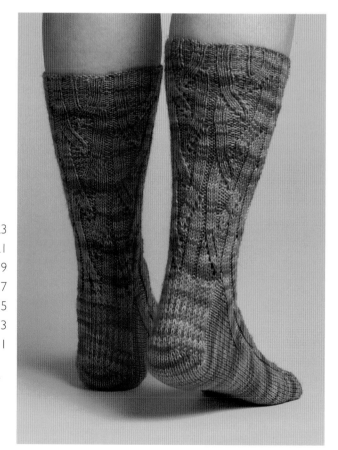

Heel

HEEL FLAP

Divide for heel flap as foll: K8, place next 34 sts on hold for top of foot; rem 31 sts will be worked back and forth for heel flap (including 8 sts from beg of rnd). Turn work so that WS is facing.

ROW 1: (WS) Sl 1 purlwise (pwise) with yarn in front (wyf), p30, turn.

ROW 2: [Sl 1 pwise with yarn in back (wyb), k1] 15 times, k1, turn. Rep Rows 1 and 2 until heel flap measures 2¼–2½" (5.5–6.5 cm) or desired length, ending after Row 1.

TURN HEEL

Work back and forth in short-rows to shape heel.

ROW 1: (RS) Sl 1 pwise wyb, k17, ssk, k1, turn.

ROW 2: Sl 1 pwise wyf, p6, p2tog, p1, turn.

ROW 3: Sl 1 pwise wyb, knit to 1 st before gap created on previous row, ssk (1 st from each side of gap), k1, turn.

ROW 4: Sl 1 pwise wyf, purl to 1 st before gap created on previous row, p2tog (1 st from each side of gap), p1, turn.

Rep Short-rows 3 and 4 until all sts have been worked—19 heel sts rem.

SHAPE GUSSET

Note: Where possible, arrange sts so that marker placement occurs between needles.

SET-UP RND: Sl 1, k8, pm for beginning of round, k10, pick up and knit 1 st in each sl st along edge of heel flap plus 1 st between heel flap and top of foot. Resume working in the rnd on held sts as foll: k1, pm for right side of foot, work 32 sts from Top of Foot chart, pm for left side of foot, knit last held st. Pick up and knit 1 st between top of foot and heel flap, pick up and knit 1 st in each sl st along edge of heel flap, k9.

RND 1: Knit to 2 st before right m, k2tog, work in next rnd of Top of Foot chart, ssk, knit to end—2 sts dec'd.

RND 2: Knit to right m, work in patt (next row from Top of Foot chart), knit to end.

Rep Rnds 1 and 2 until 65 sts rem (32 sts for top of foot and 33 sts for sole).

Foot

Work even in patt until foot measures 2" (5 cm) less than desired finished length from back of heel.

Remove m for beginning of rnd, knit to 3 sts before right m, k2tog, k1 (new beg of rnd)—64 sts rem.

Toe

RND 1: Knit.

RND 2: K1, ssk, knit to 3 sts before left m, k2tog, k1, sl m, k1, ssk, knit to 3 sts before right m, k2tog, k1—4 sts dec'd.

Rep Rnds 1 and 2 eleven more times—16 sts rem. Divide sts evenly over 2 needles so that there are 8 sts each for top of foot and sole.

Finish

Cut yarn, leaving a 12" (30 cm) tail. With tail threaded on a tapestry needle, use the Kitchener st (see Glossary) to graft sts. Weave in ends.

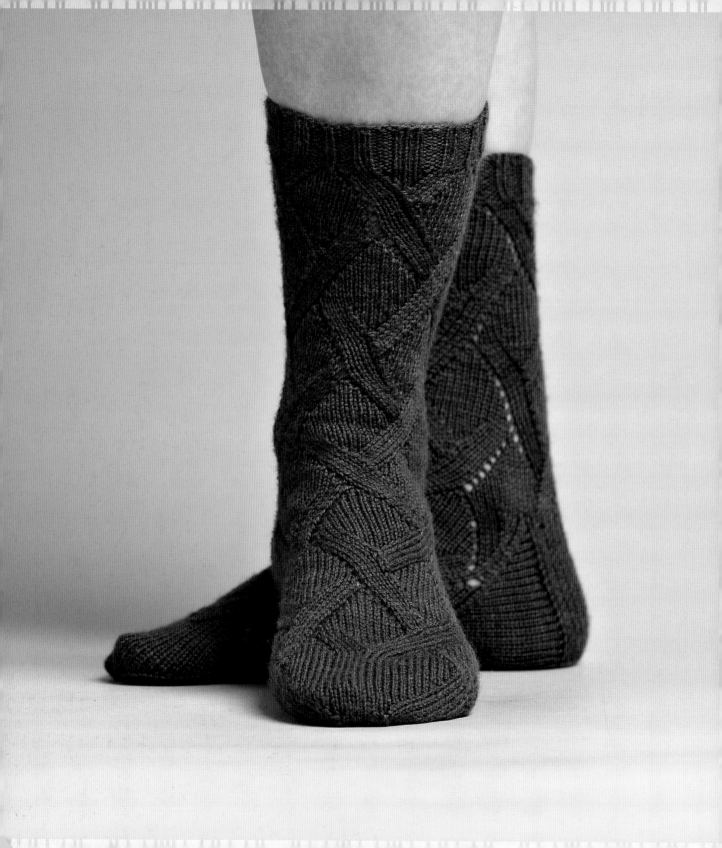

I have my Aunt Wanida to thank for teaching me to knit. She was a home economics teacher and skilled in all sorts of crafting. These socks are a perfect tribute to her because while they look simple, the diamond pattern makes these one of the most difficult pairs to design. Figuring out that two (yes, two!) jogs were needed and exactly where to place them was a labor. Once that was done, everything fell into place.

Finished Measurements

Leg circumference—8" (20.5 cm), slightly stretched.
Foot circumference—8" (20.5 cm), slightly stretched.

Yarn

Fingering weight (#1 Super Fine).
Shown here: Shelridge Farm Soft Touch Ultra
    Fingering (100% wool; 175 yd [160 m]/50 g):
    plum, 2 skeins.

Needles

U.S. size 1 (2.25 mm): circular (cir) or double-
    pointed (dpn). Adjust needle size if necessary to
    obtain the correct gauge.

Notions

Stitch markers (m; optional); tapestry needle.

Gauge

32 stitches and 48 rounds = 4" (10 cm) in stockinette
    stitch in the round.
32 stitches and 48 rounds = 4" (10 cm) in pattern in
    the round, slightly stretched.

Sizing

To resize this pattern, draw the lines created by
    increases and decreases. The inner diamond can
    be enlarged or shrunk (similar to the example on
    page 47), or the width of the spacing between the
    diamonds can be altered.

Cuff

RIBBING

CO 64 sts. Being careful not to twist sts, join for working in the round and place marker (pm) for beg of rnd.

Work Ribbing chart for 1" (2.5 cm).

Leg

Work Rnds 1–32 of Leg chart. Work Rnds 1–32 again, but *do not* shift beg of rnd at end of Rnd 32.

Heel

HEEL FLAP

Divide for heel flap as foll: Place previous 33 sts on hold for top of foot; rem 31 sts will be worked back and forth for heel flap.

ROW 1: (WS) Sl 1 purlwise (pwise) with yarn in front (wyf), p30, turn.

ROW 2: [Sl 1 pwise with yarn in back (wyb), k1] 15 times, k1, turn.

Rep Rows 1 and 2 until heel flap measures 2¼–2½" (5.5–6.5 cm) or desired length, ending after Row 1.

Leg
(multiple of 16 sts; 32 rnds)

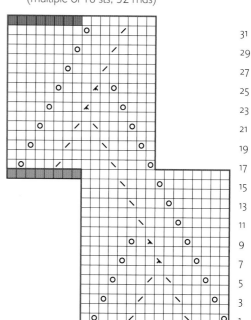

Ribbing
(multiple of 16 sts; 1 rnd rep)

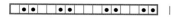

☐ Knit   ☑ K2tog   ◪ K3tog

⬤ Purl   ◩ Ssk   ◪ Sssk

◉ Yarnover   Ⓜ Make 1   ☐ Pattern repeat

▦ These sts are included in the pattern rep, BUT omit these sts from the last rep and end rnd early, shifting beg of rnd to the right.

▦ These sts are NOT included in the pattern rep. Work these sts at the end of rnd only, shifting beg of rnd to the left.

TURN HEEL

Work back and forth in short-rows to shape heel.

SHORT-ROW 1: (RS) Sl 1 pwise wyb, k17, ssk, k1, turn.

SHORT-ROW 2: Sl 1 pwise wyf, p6, p2tog, p1, turn.

SHORT-ROW 3: Sl 1 pwise wyb, knit to 1 st before gap created on previous row, ssk (1 st from each side of gap), k1, turn.

SHORT-ROW 4: Sl 1 pwise wyf, purl to 1 st before gap created by previous row, p2tog (1 st from each side of gap), p1, turn.

Rep Short-rows 3 and 4 until all sts have been worked—19 heel sts rem.

SHAPE GUSSET

Note: Where possible, arrange sts so that marker placement occurs between needles.

SET-UP RND: Sl 1 pwise wyb, k8, pm for beginning of round, k10, pick up and knit 1 st in each sl st along edge of heel flap plus 1 st between heel flap and top of foot, pm to indicate right side of foot, resume working in the rnd on held sts by working Rnd 1 of Top of Foot chart, pm for left side of foot, pick up and knit 1 st between top of foot and of heel flap and 1 st in each sl st along edge of heel flap, k9 to end of round.

RND 1: Knit to 2 sts before right m, k2tog, work next rnd from Top of Foot chart, ssk, knit to end—2 sts dec'd.

RND 2: Knit to right m, work next rnd from Top of Foot chart, knit to end.

Rep Rnds 1 and 2 until 62 sts rem (33 sts for top of foot and 29 sts for sole).

Foot

Work even in patt until foot measures 2" (5 cm) less than desired length from back of heel.

Sl first and last sts from top of foot to sole—31 sts each for top of foot and sole.

Toe

Remove m for beginning of round, knit to right m (this is the new beg of rnd).

Top of Foot
(panel of 33 sts; 32 rnd rep)

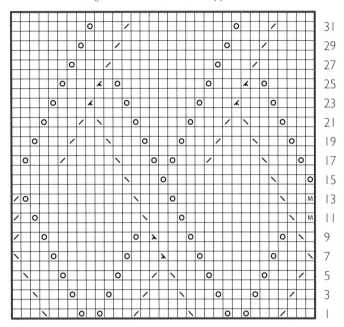

RND 1: Knit.

RND 2: K1, ssk, knit to 3 sts before left m, k2tog, k1, sl m, k1, ssk, knit to 3 sts before m indicating right side of foot, k2tog, k1—4 sts dec'd.

Rep Rnds 1 and 2 ten more times—18 sts rem. Divide sts evenly over 2 needles so that there are 9 sts each for top of foot and sole.

Finish

Cut yarn, leaving a 12" (30.5 cm) tail. With tail threaded on a tapestry needle, use the Kitchener st (see Glossary) to graft sts. Weave in ends.

sam

My father is a happy straightforward man with simple pleasures in life—walking, Tai Chi, fresh fruit, and spending time with old friends. But when I listen to stories of his youth I am always surprised by his daring, from riding a motorcycle to escaping communist China through the mountains. Like his life, these socks start with a bit of traveling (cables) and lots of texture but transition to the ease and simplicity of a stockinette foot.

Finished Measurements
Leg circumference—8" (20.5 cm), slightly stretched.
Foot circumference—8" (20.5 cm), slightly stretched.

Yarn
Fingering weight (Super Fine #1).
Shown here: Fleece Artist 2/6 Merino (100% superwash Merino; 383 yd [350 m]/115 g): Polar Sea, 1 skein.

Needles
U.S. size 1 (2.25 mm): circular (cir) or double-pointed (dpn). Adjust needle size of necessary to obtain the correct gauge.

Notions
Cable needle (cn); markers (m; optional); tapestry needle.

Gauge
32 stitches and 46 rounds = 4" (10 cm) in stockinette stitch in the round.
48 stitches and 51 rounds = 4" (10 cm) in pattern in the round, slightly stretched.

Sizing
To resize these socks, add or remove repeats, and change needle size for fine tuning.

stitch guide

Cable 2K R 2K

Sl 2 sts to cn and hold in back, k2, k2 from cn.

Cable 2K L 2K

Sl 2 sts to cn and hold in front, k2, k2 from cn.

Cable 2R Dec2

Sl 2 sts to cn and hold in back, [knit 1 st from cn together with 1 st from left needle] two times—2 sts dec'd.

Ribbing
(multiple of 8 sts; 1 rnd rep)

☐	Knit on RS, purl on WS
•	Purl on RS, knit on WS
☒	Knit into front, back, front of same st
■	No stitch
☒	Slip st pwise wyb on RS, wyf on WS
⬜	Cable 2K R 2K
⬜	Cable 2K L 2K
◣	Cable 2R Dec2
☐	Pattern repeat
▦	These sts are included in the pattern rep, BUT omit these sts from the last rep and end rnd early, shifting beg of rnd to the right.
▨	These sts are NOT included in the pattern rep. Work these sts at the end of rnd only, shifting beg of rnd to the left.

Set-up
(multiple of 8 sts inc'd to 12 sts; 11 rnds)

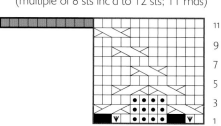

Cuff
RIBBING

CO 64 sts. Being careful not to twist stitches, for working in the round and place marker (pm) for beg of rnd.

Work Ribbing chart for 1" (2.5 cm).

SET UP FOR LEG

Work Rnds 1–11 of Set-up chart—96 sts.

At the end of Rnd 11, remove m, k10, pm for new beginning of round.

Leg

RND 1: Work Rnd 1 from Leg chart to end of rnd (8 repeats).

RND 2: Work Rnd 2 of Leg chart to m, remove m, k2, pm for new beginning of round.

RNDS 3–11: Work in patt following Leg chart.

RND 12: Knit to 10 sts before m, pm here for new beginning of round (remove later m).

RND 13: Work in patt following Leg chart.

RND 14: Knit to 2 sts before m, pm for new beg of rnd (remove later m).

RNDS 15–23: Work in patt following Leg chart.

RND 24: Work Row 24 from Leg chart. Shift beg of rnd 10 stitches to the left by removing m, k10, and pm for new beg of rnd.

Rep Rnds 1–24 two times, then work Rnds 1–3 once more.

Heel
HEEL FLAP

Divide for heel flap as foll: Place next 48 sts on hold for top of foot; rem 48 sts will be worked back and forth for heel flap. Turn work so that WS is facing.

Beg with a WS row and reading Row 1 and all WS rows from left to right, work Rows 1–6 of Heel Flap chart (page 94) back and forth in rows—32 sts rem. Rep Rows 5 and 6 until heel flap measures 2¼–2½" (5.5–6.5 cm) or desired length, ending after Row 5.

TURN HEEL

Work back and forth in short-rows to shape heel.

SHORT-ROW 1: (RS): Sl 1 purlwise (pwise) with yarn in back (wyb), k18, ssk, k1, turn.

SHORT-ROW 2: Sl 1 pwise with yarn in front (wyf), p7, p2tog, p1, turn.

SHORT-ROW 3: Sl 1 pwise wyb, knit to 1 st before gap created on previous row, ssk (1 st from each side of gap), k1, turn.

SHORT-ROW 4: Sl 1 pwise wyf, purl to 1 st before gap created on previous row, p2tog (1 st from each side of gap), p1, turn.

Rep Short-rows 3 and 4 until all sts have been worked—20 heel sts rem.

Leg
(multiple of 12 sts; 24 rnd rep; beginning of round shifts)

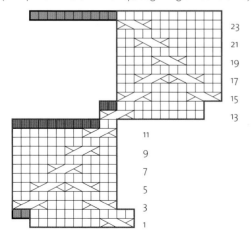

Heel Flap

(panel of 48 sts dec'd to 32 sts; 6 rows)

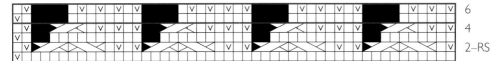

6

4

2–RS

Top of Foot

(panel of 48 sts dec'd to 32 sts; 4 rows)

4

2–RS

SHAPE GUSSETS

SET-UP RND: Sl 1 pwise wyb, k9, pm for beginning of round, k10, pick up and knit (see Glossary) 1 st in each sl st along edge of heel flap plus 1 st between heel flap and top of foot, pm for right side of foot, resume working in the rnd over held sts by working Rnd 1 of Top of Foot chart, pm for left side of foot, pick up and knit 1 st between top of foot and heel flap and 1 st in each sl st along edge of heel flap, k10 to end of round.

RND 1: Knit to 2 sts before right m, k2tog, work Rnd 2 of Top of Foot chart to left m, sl m, ssk, knit to end—10 stitches dec'd.

RND 2: Knit to right m, sl m, work Rnd 3 from Top of Foot chart to left m, sl m, knit to end.

RND 3: Knit to 2 sts before right m, k2tog, sl m, work Rnd 4 of Foot chart to left m, sl m, ssk, knit to end—10 sts dec'd.

RND 4: Knit.

RND 5: Knit to 2 sts before right m, k2tog, sl m, k32, ssk, knit to end—2 sts dec'd.

Rep Rnds 4 and 5 until 64 sts rem (32 sts each for top of foot and sole).

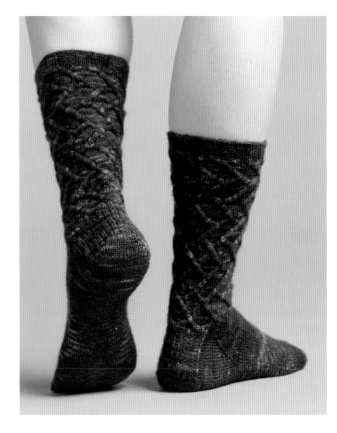

Foot

Work even in St st until foot measures 2" (5 cm) less than desired length from back of heel. Remove m for beg of rnd, knit to right m (new beg of rnd).

Toe

RND 1: Knit.

RND 2: K1, ssk, knit to 3 sts before left m, k2tog, k1, k1, ssk, knit to 3 sts before m, k2tog, k1.

Rep Rnds 1 and 2 eleven more times, then rep Rnd 1 once more—16 sts rem. Divide sts evenly over 2 needles so that there are 8 sts each for top of foot and sole.

Finishing

Cut yarn, leaving a 12" (30.5 cm) tail. With tail threaded on a tapestry needle, use the Kitchener st (see Glossary) to graft sts. Weave in ends.

ex is an artist pal of mine who likes androgyny and a good rant; these socks combine those elements. The increases needed to transition from the cast-on edge to the heavily cabled texture are spread out over two rounds; the decreases to transition from the cabled texture to the slipped-stitch-heel pattern span two rows. The stitch pattern is staggered horizontally, and the top of the foot cuts into some cables that are converted to plain stitches.

Finished Measurements

Leg circumference—8" (20.5 cm), slightly stretched.
Foot circumference—8" (20.5 cm), slightly stretched.

Yarn

Fingering weight (Super Fine #1).
Shown here: Lana Grossa Meilenweit Seta/Cashmere
(65% wool, 15% silk, 16% polyamide, 4%
cashmere; 209 yd [191 m]/50 g): #10 light gray,
3 balls.

Needles

U.S. size 1 (2.25 mm): circular (cir) or double-
pointed (dpn). Adjust needle size of necessary to
obtain the correct gauge.

Notions

Two cable needles (cn); markers (m; optional);
tapestry needle.

Gauge

32 stitches and 48 rounds = 4" (10 cm) in stockinette
stitch in the round.
44 stitches and 46 rounds = 4" (10 cm) in pattern in
the round, slightly stretched.

Sizing

This stitch pattern may look complex, but when
deconstructed into smaller elements (see page 49),
each piece is easy to resize.

stitch guide

Rib Cross 3L

Sl 3 sts to first cn and hold in front; sl 1 st to second cn and hold in back; k1 tbl, p1, k1 tbl; p1 from second cn; [k1 tbl, p1, k1 tbl] from first cn.

Rib Cross 3L Dec4

Sl 3 sts to cn and hold in front; knit 1 st from cn together with 2 sts from left needle tbl (2 sts dec'd), purl 1 st from left needle together with stitch from cn (1 st dec'd), knit 1 from cn together with 1 st from left needle tbl (1 st dec'd)—4 sts dec'd total.

Cable 1P L 1K tbl

On RS: Sl 1 st to cn and hold in front, p1, k1 tbl from cn.
On WS: Sl 1 st to cn and hold in front, p1 tbl, k1 from cn.

Cable 1K tbl R 1P

On RS: Sl 1 st to cn and hold in back, k1 tbl, p1 from cn.
On WS: Sl 1 st to cn and hold in back, k1, p1 tbl from cn.

Cable 1K tbl L 1K tbl

On RS: Sl 1 st to cn and hold in front, k1 tbl, k1 tbl from cn.
On WS: Sl 1 st to cn and hold in front, p1 tbl, p1 tbl from cn.

Cable 1K tbl R 1K tbl

On RS: Sl 1 st to cn and hold in back, k1 tbl, k1 tbl from cn.
On WS: Sl 1 st to cn and hold in back, p1 tbl, p1 tbl from cn.

Cable 1K L 1K tbl

On RS: Sl 1 st to cn and hold in front, k1, k1 tbl from cn.
On WS: Sl 1 st to cn and hold in front, p1 tbl, p1 from cn.

Cable 1K tbl R 1K

On RS: Sl 1 st to cn and hold in back, k1 tbl, k1 from cn.
On WS: Sl 1 st to cn and hold in back, p1, p1 tbl from cn.

Cuff

CO 64. Being careful not to twist stitches, join for working in the round and place marker (pm) for beg of rnd.

Work Rnds 1–14 of Set-up chart—88 sts.

Leg

Work Rnds 1–29 of Leg chart.

RND 30: Work Rnd 30 of Leg chart to last 11 sts, pm for new beg of rnd (remove later m).

Rep Rnds 1–30, again shifting m for beg of rnd 11 stitches to the right. Rep Rnds 1–12 once more.

☐	Knit on RS, purl on WS
℞	Knit tbl on RS, purl tbl on WS
•	Purl on RS, knit on WS
P	M1P
V	Slip st purlwise wyb on RS, wyf on WS
■	No stitch
☑	K2tog on RS, p2tog on WS
◹	Ssk on RS, ssp on WS
�	Kfbfbf
⧄	Cable 1K tbl R 1K tbl
⧄	Cable 1K tbl R 1P
⧄	Cable 1K tbl R K1
⧅	Cable 1K tbl L 1K tbl
⧅	Cable 1P L 1K tbl
⧅	Cable 1K L K tbl
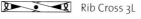	Rib Cross 3L
	Rib Cross 3L Dec4
☐	Pattern repeat
▦	These sts are included in the pattern rep, BUT omit these sts from the last rep and end rnd early, shifting beg of rnd to the right.

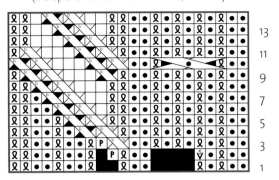

Heel

HEEL FLAP

Divide for heel flap as foll: Place next 44 sts on hold for top of foot; rem 44 sts will be worked back and forth for heel flap. Turn work so that WS is facing.

Beg with a WS row and reading Row 1 and all WS rows from left to right, work Rows 1–10 of Heel Flap chart—36 sts rem. Rep Rows 9 and 10 until heel flap measures 2¼–2½" (5.5–6.5 cm) or desired length, ending after Row 9.

TURN HEEL

Work back and forth in short-rows to shape heel.

SHORT-ROW 1: (RS): Sl 1 purlwise (pwise) with yarn in back (wyb), k20, ssk, k1, turn.

SHORT-ROW 2: Sl 1 pwise with yarn in front (wyf), p7, p2tog, p1, turn.

SHORT-ROW 3: Sl 1 pwise wyb, knit to 1 st before gap created on previous row, ssk (1 st from each side of gap), k1, turn.

SHORT-ROW 4: Sl 1 pwise wyf, purl to 1 st before gap created on previous row, p2tog (1 st from each side of gap), p1, turn.

Rep Short-rows 3 and 4 until all sts have been worked—22 heel sts rem.

Leg
(multiple of 22 sts; 30 rnd rep)

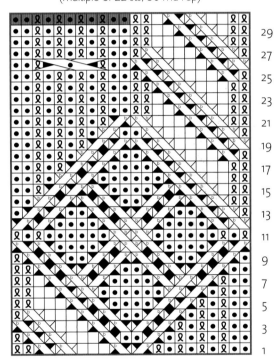

Heel Flap
(panel of 44 sts dec'd to 36 sts; 10 rows)

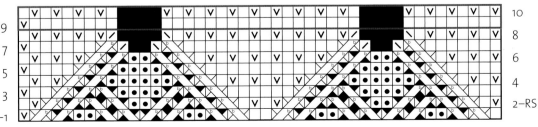

Top of Foot
(panel of 44 sts; 46 rnds)

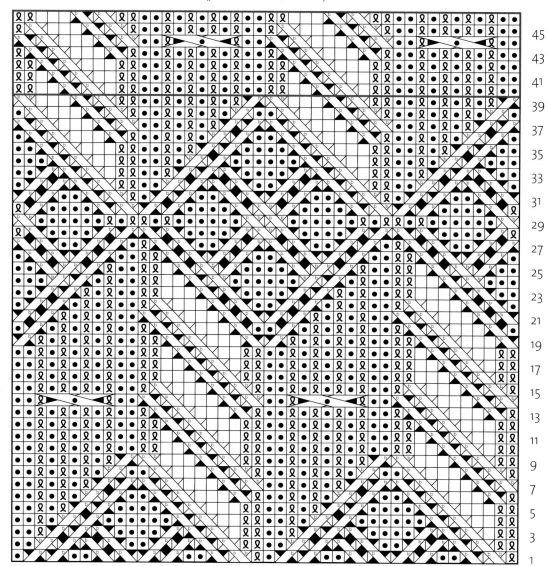

45
43
41
39
37
35
33
31
29
27
25
23
21
19
17
15
13
11
9
7
5
3
1

Decrease Round
(panel of 44 sts dec'd to 32 sts; 1 rnd)

44

SHAPE GUSSETS

Note: Where possible, arrange sts so that marker placement occurs between rnds.

SET-UP RND: Sl 1 pwise wyb, k10, pm for beginning of round, k11, pick up and knit (see Glossary) 1 st in each sl st along edge of heel flap plus 1 st between heel flap and top of foot, pm for right side of foot, resume working in the rnd on held sts by working Rnd 1 from Top of Foot chart, pm for left side of foot, k1, pick up and knit 1 st between top of foot and heel flap and in each sl st along edge of heel flap; k11 to end of round.

RND 1: Knit to 2 sts before right m, k2tog, sl m, work next rnd of Top of Foot chart to left m, sl m, ssk, knit to beginning of rnd m—2 sts dec'd.

RND 2: Knit to right m, work next rnd of Top of Foot chart to left m, sl m, knit to beginning of rnd m.

Rep Rnds 1 and 2 until 76 sts rem (44 sts for top of foot and 32 sts for sole).

Foot

Work in patt as established, repeating Rnds 40–46 as needed, until foot measures about but not more than 2" (5 cm) less than desired length from back of heel, ending after Rnd 43.

NEXT RND: (dec rnd) Knit to right m, work Decrease Round chart to left m, sl m, knit to beg of rnd m—64 sts rem (32 sts each for top of foot and sole).

If necessary, work even in St st until foot measures 2" (5 cm) less than desired length from back of heel.

Toe

Remove m for beg of rnd, knit to right m (new beg of rnd).

RND 1: Knit.

RND 2: K1, ssk, knit to 3 sts before left m, k2tog, k1, sl m, k1, ssk, knit to 3 sts before m indicating right side of foot, k2tog, k1—4 sts dec'd.

Rep Rnds 1 and 2 eleven more times—16 sts rem. Divide sts evenly over 2 needles so that there are 8 sts each for top of foot and sole.

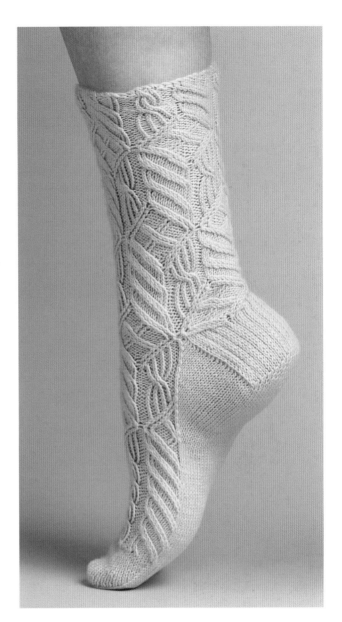

Finish

Cut yarn, leaving a 12" (30.5 cm) tail. With tail threaded on a tapestry needle, use the Kitchener st (see Glossary) to graft sts. Weave in ends.

My first cat was named after the French mathematician Augustin Louis Cauchy (koh-shee), who was famous for the Cauchy-Schwarz inequality among numerous other accomplishments. These socks use a simple knit/purl combination to form lines that resemble inequality signs, hence the name. I paired it with a picot cuff, but a simple 1×1 or 2×2 ribbed cuff would give them a more man-friendly style.

Finished Measurements

Leg circumference—8" (20.5 cm), slightly stretched.
Foot circumference—8" (20.5 cm), slightly stretched.

Yarn

Fingering weight (Super Fine #1).
Shown here: Louet Gems Fingering Weight (100% superwash Merino; 185 yd [169 m]/50 g): Pewter, 2 skeins.

Needles

U.S. size 1 (2.25 mm) and 1½ (2.5 mm): circular (cir) or double-pointed (dpn). Adjust needle size of necessary to obtain the correct gauge.

Notions

Markers (m; optional); tapestry needle.

Gauge

32 stitches and 45 rounds = 4" (10 cm) in stockinette stitch in the round with larger needles.
30 stitches and 49 rounds = 4" (10 cm) in pattern in the round, slightly stretched, with larger needles.

Sizing

This pattern is fairly straightforward, with an even number of repeats, and could be resized by widening and lengthening the knit/purl areas.

Cuff

Using smaller needles and provisional method (see Glossary), CO 60 sts. Being careful not to twist sts, join for working in the round and place marker (pm) for beg of rnd.

RNDS 1–6: Work in stockinette stitch.

RND 7: (picot rnd) *Yo, k2tog; rep from * to end.

RND 8–13: With larger needles, work in stockinette stitch. Remove provisional CO and place revealed sts on smaller needles and fold cuff at picot rnd.

RND 14: [K1 from larger needle together with 1 st from smaller needle] to end—60 sts.

Leg

Work Set-up chart for 2 rnds.

Work Pattern chart until sock measures 6" (18 cm) from fold of picot edge.

Set-up
(multiple of 10 sts; 2 rnds)

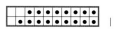

☐ Knit
⊡ Purl
☐ Pattern repeat

Pattern
(multiple of 10 sts; 28 rnd rep)

27
25
23
21
19
17
15
13
11
9
7
5
3
1

Heel

HEEL FLAP

Divide for heel flap as foll: Place prev 31 stitches on hold for top of foot; rem 29 sts will be worked back and forth for heel flap.

ROW 1: (RS) [Sl 1 purlwise (pwise) with yarn in back (wyb), k1] 14 times, k1, turn.

ROW 2: Sl 1 pwise with yarn in front (wyf), p28, turn.

Rep Rows 1 and 2 until heel flap measures 2¼–2½" (5.5–6.5 cm) or desired length, ending after Row 2.

TURN HEEL

Work back and forth in short-rows to shape heel.

SHORT-ROW 1: (RS) Sl 1 pwise wyb, k15, ssk, k1, turn.

SHORT-ROW 2: Sl 1 pwise wyf, p4, p2tog, p1, turn.

SHORT-ROW 3: Sl 1 pwise wyb, knit to 1 st before gap created on previous row, ssk (1 st from each side of gap), k1, turn.

SHORT-ROW 4: Sl 1 pwise wyf, purl to 1 st before gap created on previous row, p2tog (1 st from each side of gap), p1, turn.

Rep Short-rows 3 and 4 until all sts have been worked—17 heel sts rem.

SHAPE GUSSETS

Note: Where possible, arrange sts so that marker placement occurs between needles.

SET-UP RND: Sl 1 pwise wyb, k7, pm for beginning of round, k9, pick up and knit (see Glossary) 1 st in each sl st along edge of heel flap plus 1 st between heel flap and top of foot, pm for right side of foot. Resume working in the rnd on held sts: k1, work Pattern chart over 30 sts, pm for left side of foot. Pick up and knit 1 st between top of foot and heel flap and 1 st in each sl st along edge of heel flap, k8 to end of round.

RND 1: Knit to 2 sts before right m, k2tog, k1, work in patt to left m, ssk, knit to end—2 sts dec'd.

RND 2: Knit to right m, k1, work in patt to left m, knit to end.

Rep Rnds 1 and 2 until 62 sts rem (31 sts each for top of foot and sole).

Foot

Work even in patt without further decreases until foot measures 2" (5 cm) less than desired length from back of heel.

Toe

Remove m for beginning of round, knit to right m (new beg of rnd).

RND 1: Knit.

RND 2: K1, ssk, knit to 3 sts before left m, k2tog, k1, sl m, k1, ssk, knit to 3 sts before right m, k2tog, k1—4 sts dec'd.

Repeat Rnds 1 and 2 ten more times—18 sts rem. Divide sts evenly over 2 needles so that there are 9 sts each for top of foot and sole.

Finish

Cut yarn, leaving a 12" (30 cm) tail. With tail threaded on a tapestry needle, use the Kitchener st (see Glossary) to graft sts. Weave in ends.

rick

My brother has always had a serious need for speed. These socks evoke aerodynamic racing stripes, combining strong diagonal lines with twisted rib. On top of the foot, the pattern intersects itself and changes direction. Right and left sock are mirrored for contoured shaping. Take care at the top of the foot. Notice how the elements line up and how the stitch count is kept even by decreasing within the vertical purl welt.

Finished Measurements
Leg circumference—8" (20.5 cm), slightly stretched.
Foot circumference—8¼" (21 cm), slightly stretched.

Yarn
Fingering weight (Super Fine #1).
Shown here: Blue Moon Fiber Arts Socks That Rock Lightweight (100% superwash Merino; 360 yd [329 m]/4.5 oz): Brick, 1 skein.

Needles
U.S. size 1½ (2.5 mm): circular (cir) or double-pointed (dpn). Adjust needle size if necessary to obtain the correct gauge.

Notions
Markers (m; optional); tapestry needle.

Gauge
32 stitches and 44 rounds = 4" (10 cm) in stockinette stitch in the round.
30 stitches and 48 rounds = 4" (10 cm) inches in pattern in the round, slightly stretched.

Sizing
Since each stitch pattern repeat is narrow, increasing or decreasing the size of the sock by adding or removing repeats is easy.

Note
Left and right socks are mirror images of each other. Each sock uses different charts (as marked). Directions are the same for both socks except where specified.

Ribbing
(multiple of 12 sts; 1 rnd rep)

Right Leg
(multiple of 12 sts; 4 rnd rep)

Left Leg
(multiple of 12 sts; 4 rnd rep)

☐ Knit

🄡 Knit tbl

• Purl

🄾 Yarnover

⟋ K2tog

⟍ Ssk

⟋ K3tog

⟍ Sssk

☐ Pattern repeat

Cuff

CO 60 sts. Being careful not to twist stitches, join for working in the round and place marker (pm) for beg of rnd.

Work Ribbing chart for 1" (2.5 cm).

Leg

Work from Leg chart for respective sock until leg measures 7" (18 cm) from CO (about 18 repeats), ending after Rnd 4.

Heel

HEEL FLAP SET-UP
Right Sock Only:

NEXT RND: [Work Rnd 1 of Leg chart] 3 times, knit to 1 st before m, remove m.

Left Sock Only:

NEXT RND: Work Row 1 of Leg Pattern chart to end of round, remove m, k5.

HEEL FLAP

Divide for heel flap as foll: Place next 32 sts on hold for top of foot; rem 28 sts will be worked back and forth for heel flap. Turn work so that WS is facing.

ROW 1: (WS) Sl 1 purlwise (pwise) with yarn in front (wyf), p27, turn.

ROW 2: [Sl 1 pwise with yarn in back (wyb), k1] 14 times, turn.

Rep Rows 1 and 2 until heel flap measures 2½" (6.5 cm), ending after Row 1.

TURN HEEL

Work back and forth in short-rows to shape heel.

SHORT-ROW 1: (RS) Sl 1 pwise wyb, k16, ssk, k1, turn.

SHORT-ROW 2: Sl 1 pwise wyf, p7, p2tog, p1, turn.

SHORT-ROW 3: Sl 1 pwise wyb, knit to 1 st before gap created on previous row, ssk (1 st from each side of gap), k1, turn.

SHORT-ROW 4: Sl 1 pwise wyf, purl to 1 st before gap created on previous row, p2tog (1 st from each side of gap), p1, turn.

Rep Short-rows 3 and 4 until all sts have been worked—18 heel sts rem.

SHAPE GUSSETS

Note: Where possible, arrange sts so that marker placement occurs between needles.

SET-UP RND: Sl 1 pwise wyb, k8, pm for beginning of round, k9, pick up and knit (see Glossary) 1 st in each sl st along edge of heel flap plus and 1 st between heel flap and top of foot, pm for right side of foot, resume working in the rnd on held sts by working Rnd 1 of Foot chart for respective sock (see page 110), pm for left side of foot, pick up and knit 1 st between top of foot and heel flap and 1 st in each sl st along edge of heel flap, k9.

RND 1: Knit to 2 sts before right m, k2tog, work in patt as established (following respective Foot chart) to left m, ssk, knit to end—2 sts dec'd.

RND 2: Knit to right m, work in patt as established, knit to m for beg of rnd.

Rep Rnds 1 and 2 until 64 sts rem (32 sts each for top of foot and sole).

Foot

Work even in patt until foot measures 2" (5 cm) less than desired length from back of heel.

Toe

Remove m for beginning of round, knit to right m (new beg of rnd).

RND 1: Knit.

RND 2: K1, ssk, knit to 3 sts before left m, k2tog, k1, sl m, k1, ssk, knit to 3 sts before right m, k2tog, k1—4 sts dec'd.

Rep Rnds 1 and 2 eleven more times—16 stitches rem. Divide sts evenly over 2 needles so that there are 8 sts each for top of foot and sole.

Finish

Cut yarn, leaving a 12" (30 cm) tail. With tail threaded on a tapestry needle, use the Kitchener stitch (see Glossary) to graft sts. Weave in ends.

Right Foot Chart
(panel of 32 sts; 57 rnds)

Left Foot Chart
(panel of 32 sts; 57 rnds)

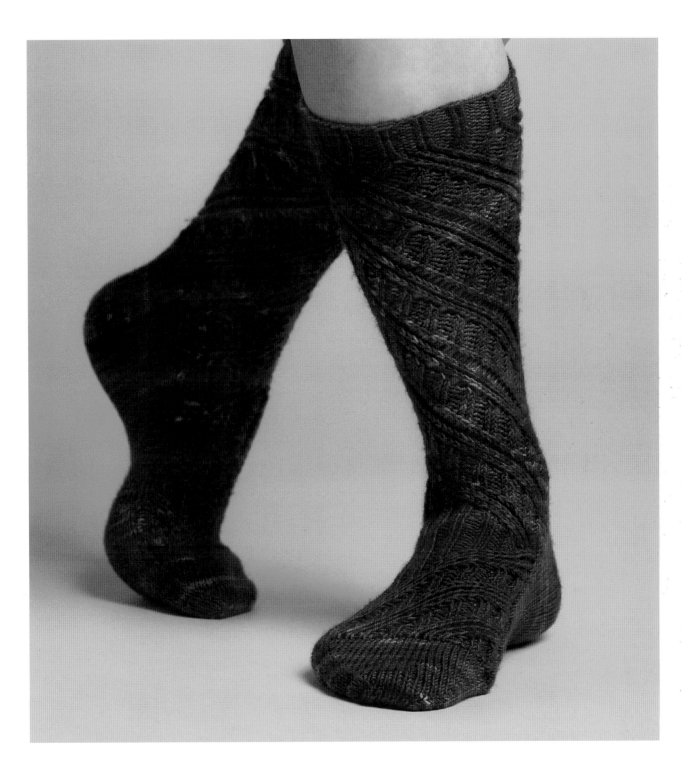

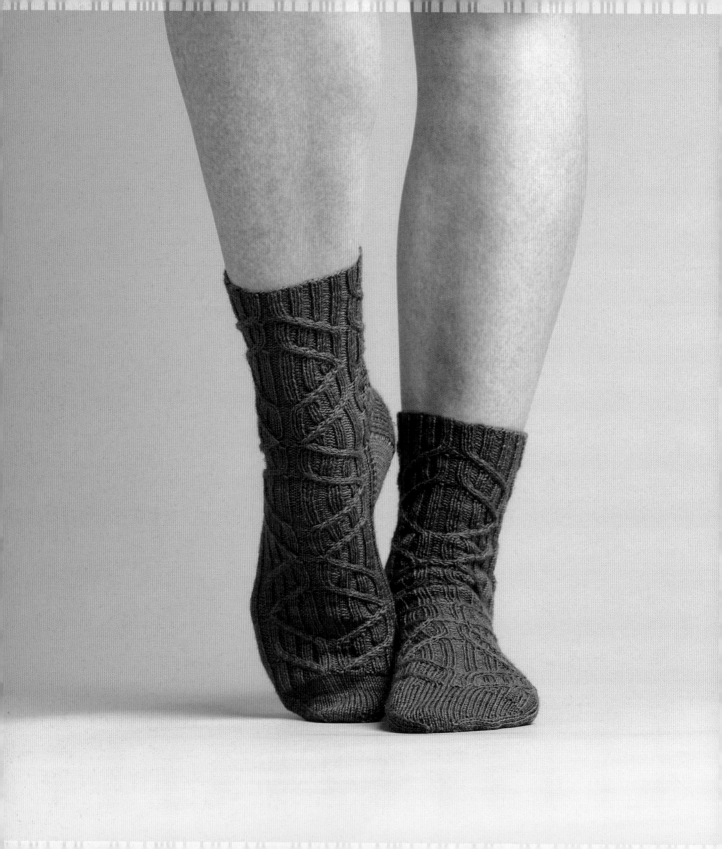

milo

ilo is a mythical creature who lives only in the minds of my husband, myself, and now possibly you. Milo cannot be described, only experienced. These socks combine vertical panels of different widths and are symmetrical down both front and back, even though the front and back are different. The cable down the back of the sock echoes the larger cable panels, weaving in and out twice each time. While the overall pattern may look complex, it is composed of smaller parts that are each much simpler.

Finished Measurements
Leg circumference—8" (20.5 cm), slightly stretched.
Foot circumference—8" (20.5 cm), slightly stretched.

Yarn
Fingering weight (Super Fine #1).
Shown here: Lorna's Laces Shepherd Sock (80% superwash wool, 20% nylon; 215 yd [197 m]/2 oz): Denim, 2 skeins.

Needles
U.S. size 1 (2.25 mm): circular (cir) or double-pointed (dpn). Adjust needle size if necessary to obtain the correct gauge.

Notions
Cable needle (cn); markers (m; optional); tapestry needle.

Gauge
32 stitches and 52 rounds = 4" (10 cm) in stockinette stitch in the round.
40 sts and 52 rounds = 4" (10 cm) in leg pattern stitch in the round.

Sizing
To resize this sock, play with the vertical purl lines between the elements.

stitch guide

Cable 2K L 2K
Sl 2 sts to cn and hold in front, k2; k2 from cn.

Cable 2K R 2K
Sl 2 sts to cn and hold in back, k2; k2 from cn.

Cable 3K L 3K
Sl 3 sts to cn and hold in front, k3; k3 from cn.

Cable 3K R 3K
Sl 3 sts to cn and hold in back, k3; k3 from cn.

Cable 2L Dec2
Sl 2 sts to cn and hold in front, [knit 1 st from cn together with 1 st from left needle] two times—2 sts dec'd.

Cable 2R Dec2
Sl 2 sts to cn and hold in back, [knit 1 st from cn together with 1 st from left needle] two times—2 sts dec'd.

Cable 3L Dec3
Sl 3 sts to cn and hold in front, [knit 1 st from cn together with 1 st from left needle] three times—3 sts dec'd.

Cable 3R Dec3
Sl 3 sts to cn and hold in back, [knit 1 st from cn together with 1 st from left needle] three times—3 sts dec'd.

Cable 2P L 2K
Sl 2 sts to cn and hold in front, p2; k2 from cn.

Cable 2K R 2P
Sl 2 sts to cn and hold in back, k2; p2 from cn.

Cuff
RIBBING
CO 72 sts. Being careful not to twist stitches, join for working in the round and place marker (pm) for beg of rnd.

Work Rnds 1–10 from Ribbing chart—78 sts.

Leg
Following Construction diagram (see page 117), work 48 rnds for leg as foll: Work Rnds 1–12 of Charts A and B *and at the same time* work Rnds 1–24 of Chart C. (See page 116 for charts.) Work leg as shown in diagram (48 rounds). Rep first 13 rnds of diagram once more.

NEXT RND: Work Chart C Decrease, Chart B Decrease, work Row 2 of Chart B, work Row 2 of Chart A, work Chart A Decrease—68 sts rem.

NEXT RND: K18.

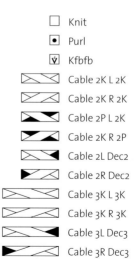

☐	Knit
⊡	Purl
⩒	Kfbfb
	Cable 2K L 2K
	Cable 2K R 2K
	Cable 2P L 2K
	Cable 2K R 2P
	Cable 2L Dec2
	Cable 2R Dec2
	Cable 3K L 3K
	Cable 3K R 3K
	Cable 3L Dec3
	Cable 3R Dec3
☐	Pattern repeat

Ribbing

(multiple of 4 sts +8 sts inc'd to 14 sts; 10 rnds)

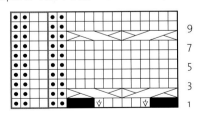

Heel

HEEL FLAP

Divide for heel flap as foll: Place next 38 sts on hold for top of foot; rem 30 sts will be worked back and forth for heel flap. Turn work so that WS is facing.

ROW 1: (WS) Sl 1 purlwise (pwise) with yarn in front (wyf), p29, turn.

ROW 2: [Sl 1 pwise with yarn in back (wyb), k1] 15 times, turn.

Rep Rows 1 and 2 until heel flap measures 2¼–2½" (5.5–6.5 cm) or desired length, ending after Row 1.

TURN HEEL

Work back and forth in short-rows to shape heel.

SHORT-ROW 1: (RS) Sl 1 pwise wyb, k16, ssk, k1, turn.

SHORT-ROW 2: Sl 1 pwise wyf, p5, p2tog, p1, turn.

SHORT-ROW 3: Sl 1 pwise wyb, knit to 1 st before gap created on previous row, ssk (1 st from each side of gap), k1, turn.

SHORT-ROW 4: Sl 1 pwise wyf, purl to 1 st before gap created on previous row, p2tog (1 st from each side of gap), p1, turn.

Rep Short-rows 3 and 4 until all sts have been worked—18 heel sts rem.

Chart A
(panel of 16 sts; 12 rnd rep)

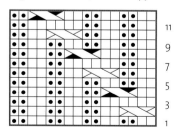

Chart B
(panel of 16 sts; 12 rnd rep)

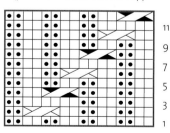

Chart A Decrease
(panel of 16 sts dec'd to 14 sts; 1 rnd)

Chart B Decrease
(panel of 16 sts dec'd to 14 sts; 1 rnd)

SHAPE GUSSETS

Note: Where possible, arrange sts so that marker placement occurs between needles.

SET-UP RND: Sl 1 pwise wyb, k8, pm for beginning of round, k9, pick up and knit (see Glossary) 1 st in each sl st along edge of heel flap plus 1 st between heel flap and top of foot. Resume working in the rnd on held sts by working k1, pm for right side of foot, k1, p2, work in patt across top of foot (Rnd 3 from Chart B, Rnd 3 from Chart A), k1, pm for left side of foot, k1. Pick up and knit 1 st between top of foot and heel flap and 1 st in each sl st along edge of heel flap, k9 to end.

RND 1: Knit to 2 st before right m, k2tog, work in patt as established to left m, ssk, knit to end—2 sts dec'd.

RND 2: Knit to right m, work in patt as established to left m, knit to end.

Rep Rnds 1 and 2 until 68 sts rem (36 sts for top of foot and 32 sts for sole).

Foot

Work even in patt without further decreases until foot measures 2" (5 cm) less than desired length from back of heel, ending after an odd-numbered chart row.

NEXT RND: Work in patt as established *except* work Cable 2L Dec2 instead of Cable 2K L 2K or Cable 2P L 2K and work Cable 2R Dec2 instead of Cable 2K R 2K or Cable 2K R 2P—64 sts rem.

Toe

Remove m for beginning of round, knit to right m (new beg of rnd).

RND 1: Knit.

RND 2: K1, ssk, knit to 3 sts before left m, k2tog, k1, k1, ssk, knit to 3 sts before right m, k2tog, k1—4 sts dec'd.

Rep Rnds 1 and 2 eleven more times—16 sts rem. Divide sts evenly over 2 needles so that there are 8 sts each for top of foot and sole.

Finish

Cut yarn, leaving a 12" (30 cm) tail. With tail threaded on a tapestry needle, use the Kitchener st (see Glossary) to graft sts. Weave in ends.

Chart C
(panel of 14 sts; 24 rnd rep)

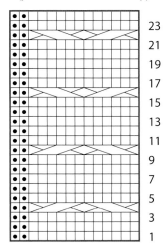

23
21
19
17
15
13
11
9
7
5
3
1

Chart C Decrease
(panel of 14 sts dec'd to 8 sts; 1 rnd)

2

Construction Diagram

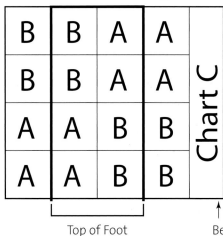

B	B	A	A
B	B	A	A
A	A	B	B
A	A	B	B

Chart C

Top of Foot

Begin here; work from right to left and bottom to top of diagram.

lindsay

These are named for my friend Lindsay, who would love to lounge around in comfy socks all day. The main stitch pattern combines garter stitch and a stockinette wedge, so the stitch count varies from round to round. On the outer side of each sock is a vertical stripe, which creates an interesting visual element and eliminates the visible jog created by garter stitch in the round. To match the garter-stitch elements of the main stitch pattern, I used a garter-stitch cuff, short-row heel, and short-row toe.

Finished Measurements
Leg circumference—8" (20.5 cm), slightly stretched.
Foot circumference—8" (20.5 cm), slightly stretched.

Yarn
Fingering weight (Super Fine #1).
Shown here: Hand Jive Knits Nature's Palette Fingering Weight (100% Merino wool; 185 yd [170 m]/50 g): Walnut, 2 skeins.

Needles
U.S. size 1 (2.25 mm): circular (cir) or double-pointed (dpn). Adjust needle size if necessary to obtain the correct gauge.

Notions
Markers (m; optional); tapestry needle.

Gauge
32 stitches and 47 rounds = 4" (10 cm) in stockinette stitch in the round.

Sizing
A simple way to resize this pattern is to play with the ribbed column, making the sock larger or smaller by expanding or contracting the ribbed section. Try adding or removing ribs or changing to a different ribbing pattern.

Note
Left and right socks are mirror images of each other. Directions are the same for both socks except where specified.

Legend

□	Knit
●	Purl
◎	Yarnover
□	Pattern repeat

☑	K2tog
◩	Ssk
◪	K4tog
◪	Ssskp
■	No stitch

Pattern
(multiple of 11 sts; 8 rnd rep)
count sts after Rnd 1 or 2

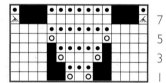

Cuff

CO 61 sts. Being careful not to twist stitches, join for working in the round and place marker (pm) for beg of rnd.

RND 1: K2, p2, k55, p2.

RND 2: K2, purl to end.

Rep Rnds 1 and 2 for 1" (2.5 cm).

Leg

SET-UP RND: K2, p2, [k3, k2tog, yo, k1, yo, ssk, k3] 5 times, p2.

NEXT RND: K2, p2, [work Pattern chart Rnd 2] 5 times, p2.

Work in patt as established following Pattern chart until piece measures 6" (15 cm) or desired length from cuff, ending after

Pattern chart Rnd 4—71 sts.

Heel
HEEL SET-UP
Right Sock only

NEXT RND: K2, p2, work Rnd 5 of Pattern chart 2 times (30 sts increased to 34 sts); heel will be worked over next 39 sts. Place rem 36 sts (2 sts from end of round and 34 sts just worked) on hold for top of foot.

Left Sock only

NEXT RND: K2, p2 (4 sts); heel will be worked over next 39 sts. Place rem 32 sts (4 sts just worked and 28 sts from end of rnd) on hold for top of foot.

SHORT-ROW GARTER-STITCH HEEL

Work back and forth in short-rows to shape heel.

SHORT-ROW 1: (RS) K37, wrap & turn (w&t); 1 unworked st at end of row.

SHORT-ROW 2: (WS) K35, w&t; 1 unworked st at end of row.

NEXT ROW: Knit to 1 st before wrapped st, w&t.

Rep last row 27 times, ending with a WS row—7 unwrapped sts, 16 wrapped sts on each side.

NEXT ROW: Knit to first wrapped st, knit wrapped st without picking up wrap, w&t (next st is wrapped twice).

Rep last row 26 times, ending with a RS row—34 sts between wrapped sts, 3 wrapped sts at end of needle (the beginning of previous row); 2 wrapped sts at tip of needle (end of previous row).

NEXT ROW: (WS) K35, w&t; 1 unworked st—2 wrapped sts at each end of needle.

NEXT ROW: (RS) K34, k3tog, do not turn—37 heel sts rem. Socks continue in the round.

Foot
Right Sock Only

SET-UP RND: Pm for beginning of rnd at right side of foot, p2, k2, p2, [work Rnd 6 from Pattern chart] 2 times, pm for left side of foot, ssk, knit to end—72 sts (36 sts each for top and bottom of foot).

NEXT RND: Work even in patt (p2, k2, p2, work next rnd from Pattern chart to left m, knit to end).

Rep last rnd until sock measures 2–2½" (5–6.5 cm) less than desired length from back of heel, ending after Rnd 2 of chart—64 sts (28 sts for top of foot, 36 sts for sole).

Move 2 sts from each edge of bottom of foot to top of foot and move markers if needed—32 sts each for top of foot and sole.

If necessary, work foll 2 rnds as needed until foot measures 2" (5 cm) less than desired length from back of heel, ending after Rnd 2:

RND 1: [K2, p2] 2 times, knit to end.

RND 2: P4, k2, purl to end.

Left Sock Only

SET-UP RND: Pm for beginning of round at right side of foot, [work row 5 from Pattern chart] 2 times, p2, k2, p2, pm for left side of foot, ssk, knit to end—72 sts (36 sts each for top of foot and sole).

NEXT RND: Work even in patt (work next rnd from Pattern chart) to 6 sts before left m, p2, k2, p2, knit to end.

Rep last rnd until sock measures 2–2½" (5–6.5 cm) less than desired length from back of heel, ending after Rnd 2 of chart—64 sts (28 sts for top of foot, 36 sts for bottom of foot).

Move 2 sts from each edge of bottom of foot to top of foot and move markers as needed—32 sts each for top and bottom of foot.

If necessary, work foll 2 rnds until foot measures 2" (5 cm) less than desired length from back of heel, ending after Rnd 2:

RND 1: Knit to 8 sts before m, [p2, k2] 2 times, knit to end.

RND 2: Purl to 6 sts before m, k2, p4, purl to end.

Toe

Note: Toe is worked in the same way as heel except it is worked over 32 sts for top of foot only.

SHORT-ROW 1: (RS) K31, w&t.

SHORT-ROW 2: K30, w&t.

NEXT ROW: Knit to 1 st before wrapped st, w&t.

Rep last row 23 times, ending after a WS row—6 unwrapped sts, 13 wrapped sts on each side.

NEXT ROW: Knit to first wrapped st, knit wrapped stitch without picking up wrap, w&t (next st is wrapped twice).

Rep last row 23 times, ending after a RS row—30 sts between wraps, 1 wrapped sts on each side.

NEXT ROW: (WS) K31 (do not wrap), turn.

Finish

Cut yarn, leaving a 12" (30 cm) tail. With tail threaded on a tapestry needle, use the Kitchener st (see Glossary) to graft toe and sole sts. Weave in ends.

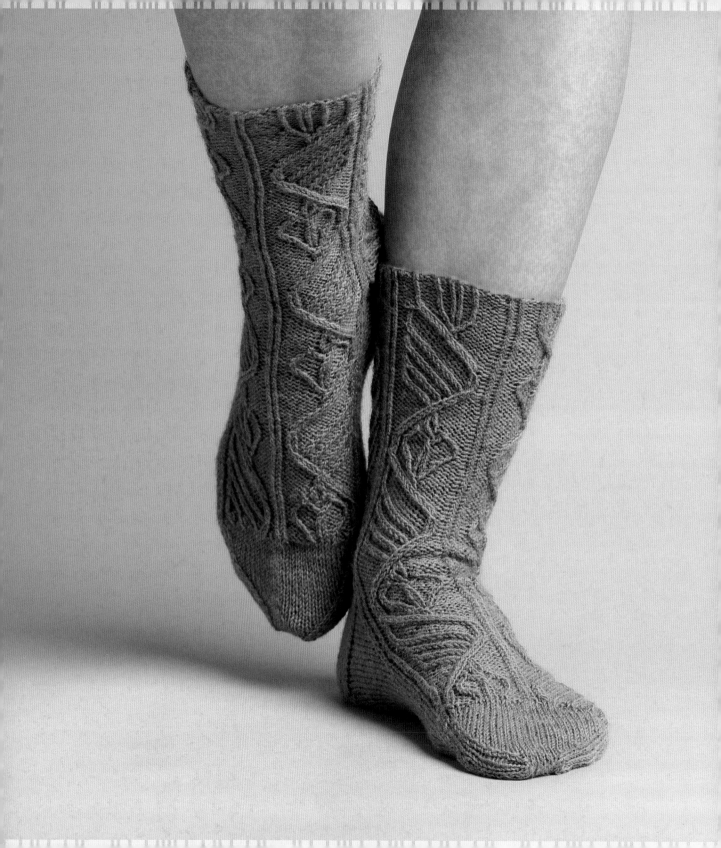

kristi

Since Kristi is my BKFF (Best Knitting Friend Forever), I pulled out all the stops. These socks use a large twisted-stitch panel, which is staggered and mirrored within each sock and across the pair. I highly recommend learning to cable without a cable needle to knit these socks more quickly. The pattern starting row allows the cuff ribbing to flow into the pattern and leaves room to space the cable increases.

Finished Measurements
Leg circumference—8" (20.5 cm), slightly stretched.
Foot circumference—8" (20.5 cm), slightly stretched.

Yarn
Fingering weight (Super Fine #1).
Shown here: Opal Uni-Color (75% superwash wool, 25% nylon; 465 yd [425 m]/100 g): #1997 Sage, 1 skein.

Needles
U.S. size 1½ (2.5 mm): circular (cir) or double-pointed (dpn). Adjust needle size if necessary to obtain the correct gauge.

Notions
Cable needle (cn), markers (m; optional); tapestry needle.

Gauge
32 stitches and 42 rounds = 4" (10 cm) in stockinette stitch in the round.
40 stitches and 44 rounds = 4" (10 cm) inches in pattern in the round, slightly stretched.

Sizing
To resize this pattern, play with the area between the main pattern panels—the [p1, k2 tbl, p1] stitches that form the vertical ridge can be reduced or expanded.

Note
Left and right socks are mirror images of each other. Directions are the same for both socks except where specified.

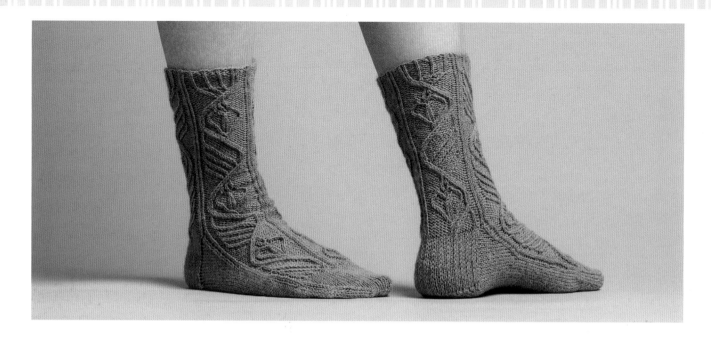

stitch guide

Cable IP L IK tbl
Sl 1 st to cn and hold in front, p1, k1 tbl from cn.
Cable IK tbl R IP
Sl 1 st to cn and hold in back, k1 tbl, p1 from cn.
Cable IP L 2K tbl
Sl 2 sts to cn and hold in front, p1, k2 tbl from cn.
Cable 2K tbl R IP
Sl 1 st to cn and hold in back, k2 tbl, p1 from cable needle.
Cable IK tbl L IK tbl
Sl 1 st to cn and hold in front, k1 tbl, k1 tbl from cn.
Cable IK tbl R IK tbl
Sl 1 st to cn and hold in back, k1 tbl, k1 tbl from cn.
Cable IK tbl L 2K tbl
Sl 2 sts to cn and hold in front, k1tbl, k2 tbl from cn.
Cable 2K tbl R IK tbl
Sl 1 st to cn and hold in back, k2 tbl, k1 tbl from cn.

Ribbing

CO 64 sts. Being careful not to twist stitches, join for working in the round and place marker (pm) for beg of rnd.

Right Sock only
Work Rnd 1 of Ribbing chart *from right to left*; rep for 1" (2.5 cm).
NEXT RND: Work Rnd 2 of Ribbing chart *from right to left*—76 sts.

Left Sock only
Work Rnd 1 of Ribbing chart *from left to right*; rep for 1" (2.5 cm).
NEXT RND: Work Rnd 2 of Ribbing chart *from left to right*—76 sts.

Leg

Right Sock only
Work Rnds 1–38 of Pattern chart, then work Rnds 1–25 again.
NEXT RND: K9, k2tog, k17, k2tog, k5, k2tog, k1—73 sts rem.

Left Sock only
Move beginning of the round 2 st to the right (by shifting stitches on the needles or moving marker).
Note: First 2 sts of pattern have already been worked as part of ribbing. For first rep of first rnd of leg only, omit first 2 sts.
  Work Rnds 20–38 of Pattern chart, then work Rnds 1–19.
Work Rnds 20–38 again, then work Rnds 1–6.
NEXT RND: K3, ssk, k5, ssk, k17, ssk, k7—73 sts rem.

Ribbing
(multiple of 32 sts inc'd to 38 sts; 2 rnds)

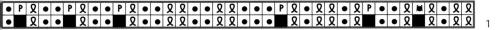

Pattern
(multiple of 38 sts; 38 rnds)

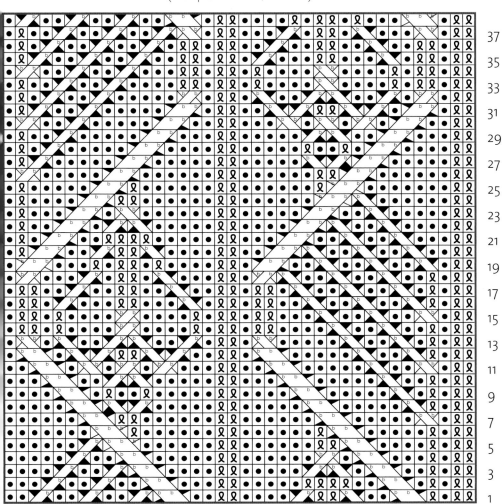

Ω	Knit tbl
•	Purl
M	M1
P	M1P
■	No stitch
□	Pattern repeat
⟋	Cable 1K tbl R 1K tbl
⟍	Cable 1K tbl L 1K tbl
⟍	Cable 1K tbl R 1P
⟍	Cable 1P L 1K tbl
⟋	Cable 2K tbl R 1K tbl
⟍	Cable 1K tbl L 2K tbl
⟋	Cable 2K tbl R 1P
⟍	Cable 1P L 2K tbl

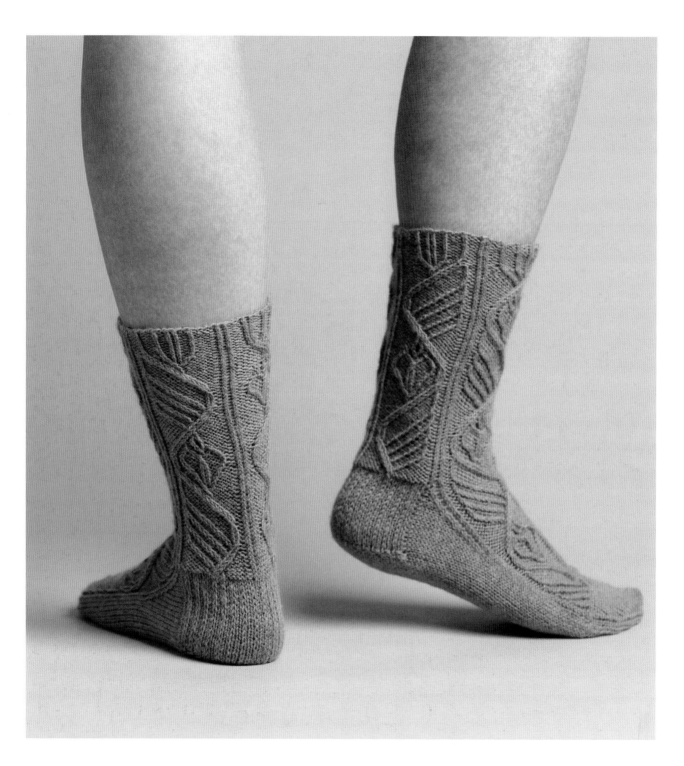

Heel

FLAP

Divide for heel flap as foll: Place next 38 sts on hold for top of foot; rem 35 sts will be worked back and forth for heel flap.

Note: First stitch of the round is held for top of foot. Turn work.

ROW 1: (WS) Sl 1 purlwise (pwise) with yarn in front (wyf), p34, turn.

ROW 2: [Sl 1 pwise with yarn in back (wyb), k1] 17 times, k1, turn.

Rep Rows 1 and 2 until heel flap measures 2¼–2½" (5.5–6.5 cm), ending after Row 1.

TURN HEEL

Work back and forth in short-rows to shape heel.

SHORT-ROW 1: (RS) Sl 1 pwise wyb, k19, ssk, k1, turn.

SHORT-ROW 2: Sl 1 pwise wyf, p6, p2tog, p1, turn.

SHORT-ROW 3: Sl 1 pwise wyb, knit to 1 st before gap created on previous row, ssk (1 st from each side of gap), k1, turn.

SHORT-ROW 4: Sl 1 pwise wyf, purl to 1 st before gap created on previous row, p2tog (1 st from each side of gap), p1, turn.

Rep Short-rows 3 and 4 until all sts have been worked—21 heel sts rem.

SHAPE GUSSETS

Note: Where possible, arrange sts so that marker placement occurs between needles.

Right Sock only

SET-UP RND: Sl 1 pwise wyb, k10, pm for beg of rnd, k10, pick up and knit (see Glossary) 1 st in each sl st along edge of heel flap plus 1 st between heel flap and top of foot, pm for right side of foot, resume working in the rnd on held sts by working Rnd 26 of Pattern chart as established, pm for left side of foot, pick up and knit 1 st between top of foot and heel flap and 1 st in each sl st along edge of heel flap, k11 to end.

Left Sock only

SET-UP RND: Sl 1 pwise wyb, k10, pm for beg of rnd, k10, pick up and knit 1 st in each sl st along edge of heel flap plus 1 st between heel flap and top of foot, pm for right side of foot, resume working in the rnd on held sts by working Rnd 7 of Pattern chart as established across top of foot sts, pm for left side of foot, pick up and knit 1 st between top of foot and heel flap and 1 st in each sl st along edge of heel flap, k11 to end.

Both Socks

RND 1: Knit to 2 st before right m, k2tog, work in patt as established to left m, sl m, ssk, knit to end—2 sts dec'd.

RND 2: Knit to right m, work in patt as established to left m, knit to end.

Rep Rnds 1 and 2 until 71 sts rem (38 sts for top of foot and 33 sts for sole).

Foot

Work even in patt without further decreases until foot measures 2" (5 cm) less than desired length from back of heel, taking note of the last rnd worked.

Knit to right m, dec 6 sts across top of foot as foll: Dec 1 st in each cable (or first and last 3 cables if there are more than 6 cables) by substituting as foll:

- For Cable 1K tbl R 1K tbl and Cable 1K tbl R 1P, work k2tog.
- For Cable 1K tbl L 1K tbl and Cable 1P L 1K tbl, work k2tog tbl.
- For Cable 2K tbl R 1K tbl and Cable 2K tbl R 1P, work k2tog, k1 tbl.
- For Cable 1K tbl L 2K tbl and Cable 1P L 2K tbl, work k1 tbl, k2tog tbl.

If there are fewer than 6 cables, dec rem sts as p2tog evenly spaced across purl background.

65 sts rem (32 sts for top of foot and 33 sts for sole).

Toe

Remove m for beginning of round, knit to 3 sts before right m, k2tog, k1, sl m (new beg of rnd)—64 sts rem.

RND 1: Knit.

RND 2: K1, ssk, knit to 3 sts before left m, k2tog, k1, k1, ssk, knit to 3 sts before right m, k2tog, k1—4 sts dec'd.

Rep Rnds 1 and 2 eleven more times—16 sts rem. Divide sts evenly over 2 needles so that there are 8 sts each for top of foot and sole.

Finish

Cut yarn, leaving a 12" (30 cm) tail. With tail threaded on a tapestry needle, use the Kitchener st (see Glossary) to graft sts. Weave in ends.

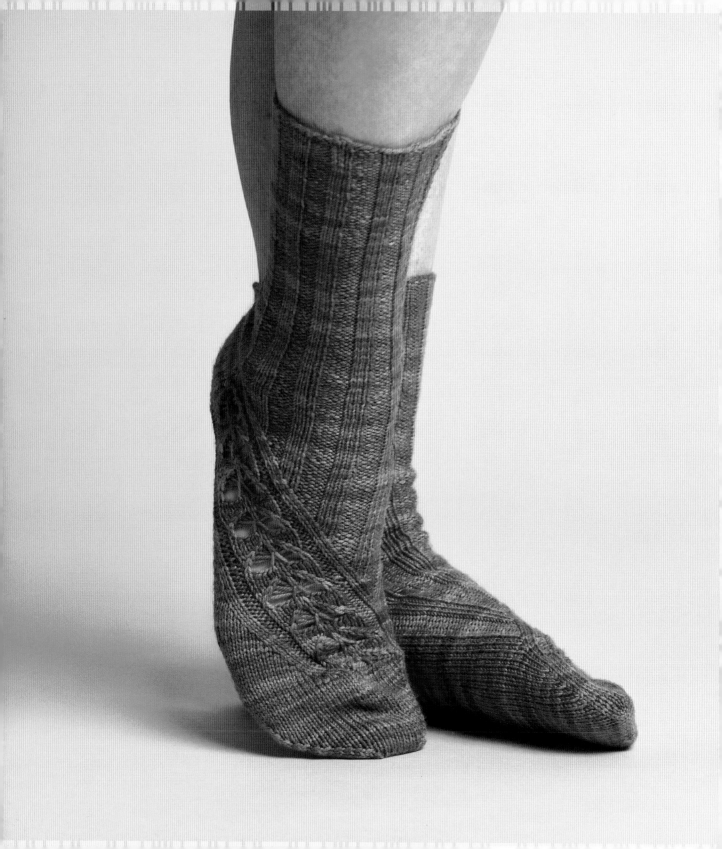

kai-mei

ai-Mei is a physicist, a mother, a feminist, and a runner to boot. Somehow she manages to put it all together. These socks combine various elements using an interesting construction. They begin with a straightforward ribbed cuff but introduce a lace pattern at the gusset stitch pick-up. Shifting the gusset decreases to one side of the lace panel causes it to angle across the top of the foot, demonstrating that the path taken need not be traditional.

Finished Measurements

Leg circumference—8" (20.5 cm), slightly stretched.
Foot circumference—8" (20.5 cm), slightly stretched.

Yarn

Fingering weight (Super Fine #1).
Shown here: Dream in Color Smooshy (100% superwash Merino wool; 450 yd [411 m]/4 oz): Happy Forest, 1 skein.

Needles

U.S. size 1 (2.25 mm): circular (cir) or double-pointed (dpn). Adjust needle size if necessary to obtain the correct gauge.

Notions

Markers (m; optional); tapestry needle.

Gauge

33 stitches and 53 rounds = 4" (10 cm) in stockinette stitch in the round.
33 stitches and 53 rounds = 4" (10 cm) in 3x3 ribbing in the round, slightly stretched.

Sizing

This pattern can be resized by adding or removing ribs in the cuff. The foot is worked the same, except the top and bottom of the foot will be narrower/wider, and the shaping will have to be shifted accordingly.

Note

Left and right socks are mirror images of each other. Directions are the same for both socks except where specified.

Leg

CO 66 sts. Being careful not to twist stitches, join for working in the round and place marker (pm) for beg of rnd.

Work k3, p3 ribbing until piece measures 6½" (16.5 cm).

Heel

HEEL FLAP

Divide for heel flap as foll: Place last 33 sts worked on hold for top of foot; rem 33 sts will be worked back and forth for heel flap.

ROW 1: (RS) [K3, p3] 5 times, k3.

ROW 2: Sl 1 purlwise (pwise) with yarn in front (wyf), p32.

ROW 3: [Sl 1 pwise with yarn in back (wyb), k1] 16 times, k1. Rep Rows 2 and 3 until heel flap measures 2¼–2½" (5.5–6.5 cm), ending after Row 2.

TURN HEEL

Work back and forth in short-rows to shape heel.

SHORT-ROW 1: (RS): Sl 1 pwise wyb, k17, ssk, k1, turn.

SHORT-ROW 2: Sl 1 pwise wyf, p4, p2tog, p1, turn.

SHORT-ROW 3: Sl 1 pwise wyb, knit to 1 st before gap created on previous row, ssk (1 st from each side of gap), k1, turn.

SHORT-ROW 4: Sl 1 pwise wyf, purl to 1 st before gap created on previous row, p2tog (1 st from each side of gap), p1, turn.

Rep Short-rows 3 and 4 until all sts have been worked—19 heel sts rem.

Panel
(panel of 15 sts; 8 rnd rep)

		Knit
☐		Knit
⦿		Purl
🝰		Pick up 4 strands of dropped yarnovers Purl 4 strands together with next stitch
◉		Yarnover. Drop yarnover on next row
◎		Yarnover 2 times. Drop yarnovers on next row
◎		Yarnover 3 times. Drop yarnovers on next row
◎		Yarnover 4 times. Drop yarnovers on next row
◣		Ssk
◢		K2tog
V		Slip stitch purlwise with yarn in back
■		No stitch
+		CO 1 stitch using backward-loop cast-on
☐		Pattern repeat

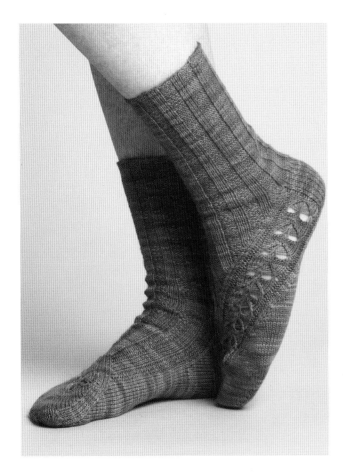

knit to end—2 sts dec'd.

RND 2: Knit to right m, work next row of Panel chart, k1, sl m, k1, work in rib patt to left m, knit to end.

RND 3: Knit to right m, work next row of Panel chart, k1, ssk, work in rib patt to left m, ssk, knit to end—2 sts dec'd.

Rep Rnds 2 and 3 until 66 sts rem.

Left Sock only

SET-UP RND: Sl 1 pwise wyb, k9, pm for beg of rnd, k9, pick up and knit 1 st in each sl st along edge of heel flap, pick up and knit 1 st between heel flap and instep, pm for right side of foot; resume working in the rnd on held sts by working [p3, k3] 5 times, p3, pick up and knit 1 st between top of foot and heel flap, pm for panel; pick up and knit 1 st in each sl st along edge of heel flap, k10 to end of round.

RND 1: Knit to 2 sts before right m, k2tog, work in rib patt to 2 sts before panel m, k2tog, k1, work Row 1 of Panel chart, pm for left side of foot, knit to end—2 sts dec'd.

RND 2: Knit to right m, sl m, work in rib patt to 1 st before panel m, k1, sl m, k1, work next row of Panel chart, sl m, knit to end.

RND 3: Knit to 2 sts before right m, k2tog, sl m, work in rib patt to 2 sts before panel m, k2tog, sl m, k1, work next row of Panel chart, sl m, knit to end—2 sts dec'd.

Rep Rnds 2 and 3 until 66 sts remain.

Foot

Right Sock only

RND 1: Knit to right m, work next rnd of Panel chart, k1, sl m, work rib patt to left m, knit to end.

RND 2: Knit to 2 sts before right m, make 1 (M1; see Glossary), k2, work next rnd of Panel chart, k1, ssk, work in rib patt to m, sl m, knit to end.

Rep Rnds 1 and 2 until foot measures 2" (5 cm) less than desired length from back of heel, ending after Rnd 1, 2, or 8 of Panel chart or when panel and left markers are separated by only 1 st.

If panel marker and left markers are separated by 1 st, remove left m. Rep Rnd 3 only until foot measures 2" (5 cm) less than desired length from back of heel, ending after Rnd 1, 2, or 8 of Panel Chart.

SHAPE GUSSETS

Note: Where possible, arrange sts so that marker placement occurs between needles.

Right Sock only

SET-UP RND: Sl 1 pwise wyb, k9, pm for beg of rnd, k9, pick up and knit 1 st in each sl st along edge of heel flap, pick up and knit 1 st between heel flap and top of foot, pm for panel; resume working in the rnd over held sts by working [p3, k3] 5 times, p3, pm for left side of foot; pick up and knit 1 st between top of foot and heel flap and 1 st in each sl st along edge of heel flap, k10 to end of round.

RND 1: Knit to 16 sts before panel m, pm for right side of foot, work Row 1 of Panel chart, k1, ssk, work rib patt to left m, ssk,

RND 3: Knit to right m, sl m, work next rnd of Panel chart, k2, sl m, k to end of round.

Left Sock only

RND 1: Knit to right m, work in rib patt to panel m, k1, work next rnd of Panel chart, sl m, knit to end.

RND 2: Knit to right m, work in rib patt to 2 sts before panel m, k2tog, k1, work next rnd of Panel chart, sl m, k2, M1, knit to end.

Rep Rnds 1 and 2 until foot measures 2" (5 cm) less than desired length from back of heel, ending after Rnd 1, 2, or 8 of Panel chart or when right and panel markers are separated by only 1 st.

If right marker and panel markers are separated by 1 st, remove panel m. Work Rnd 3 until foot measures 2" (5 cm) less than desired length from back of heel, ending after Rnd 1, 2, or 8 of Panel Chart.

RND 3: Knit to right m, k2, work next rnd of Panel chart, knit to end.

Toe

Right Sock only

Remove all m except for left m, count 33 sts from left m, and pm for new right side/beginning of round. Knit to right m.

Left Sock only

Remove all m except for right m, count 33 sts from right m, and pm for new left side. Knit to right m (new beg of rnd).

Both Socks

RND 1: Knit.

RND 2: K1, ssk, knit to 3 sts before left m, k2tog, k1, k1, ssk, knit to 3 sts before right m, k2tog, k1—4 sts dec'd.

Rep Rnds 1 and 2 eleven more times—18 sts rem. Divide sts evenly over 2 needles so that there are 9 sts each for top of foot and sole.

Finish

Cut yarn, leaving a 12" (30 cm) tail. With tail threaded on a tapestry needle, use the Kitchener st (see Glossary) to graft sts. Weave in ends.

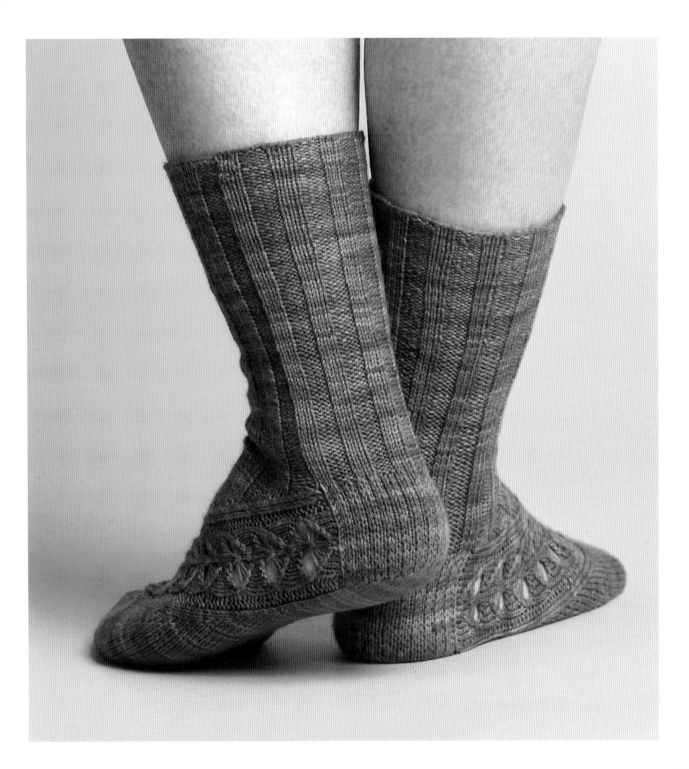

beg	beginning; begin; begins	**RS**	right side
BO	bind off	**sl**	slip
CC	contrasting color	**sl st**	slip st (slip 1 st pwise unless otherwise indicated)
cm	centimeter(s)	**ssk**	slip 2 sts kwise, one at a time, from the left to
cn	cable needle		right needle, insert left needle tip through both
CO	cast on		front loops and knit together from this position
dec(s)	decrease(s); decreasing		(1 st dec'd)
dpn	double-pointed needles	**ssp**	slip 2 sts kwise, one at a time, from left to right
g	gram(s)		needle, sl these sts tog back to left needle pwise,
inc(s)	increase(s); increasing		purl these sts tog through their back loops (1 st
k	knit		dec'd)
k1f&b	knit into the front and back of same st	**sssp**	slip 3 sts kwise, one at a time, from left to right
kfbf	knit into the [front, back, front] of the same stitch		needle, sl these sts tog back to left needle pwise,
	(2 sts inc'd)		purl these sts tog through their back loops (2 sts
kfbfb	knit into the [front, back, front, back] of the same		dec'd)
	stitch (3 sts inc'd)	**St st**	stockinette stitch
kwise	knitwise, as if to knit	**tbl**	through back loop
left leg	the side of the stitch closest to the unworked sts	**tog**	together
	on the left needle; typically falls behind left needle	**WS**	wrong side
m	marker(s)	**wyb**	with yarn in back
MC	main color	**wyf**	with yarn in front
mm	millimeter(s)	**yd**	yard(s)
M1	make one (increase)	**yo**	yarn over
p	purl	*****	repeat starting point
p1f&b	purl into front and back of same st	*** ***	repeat all instructions between asterisks
patt(s)	pattern(s)	**( )**	alternate measurements and/or instructions
psso	pass slipped st over	**[ ]**	instructions are worked as a group a specified
pwise	purlwise, as if to purl		number of times
rem	remain; remaining		
rep	repeat(s)		
rev St st	reverse stockinette stitch		
right leg	the side of the stitch closest to the completed sts		
	or tip of left needle; typically falls in front of left		
	needle		
rnd(s)	round(s)		

Cast-Ons

BACKWARD-LOOP CAST-ON

*Loop working yarn and place it on needle backward so that it doesn't unwind. Repeat from *.

EASTERN CAST-ON

Hold two dpn parallel to each other. Leaving a 6" (15 cm) tail, wrap the working yarn around both needles counterclockwise **(Figure 1)** half as many times as the number of stitches you want. For example, if you want to cast on 12 stitches, wrap the yarn around the two needles six times. To begin, bring the yarn forward between the two needles and use a third needle to knit across the wraps on the top needle **(Figure 2)**. Rotate the two needles so that the needle that had been on the bottom is now on the top; use the free needle to knit across the wraps on that needle **(Figure 3)**. (Can be used as a provisional cast-on by continuing to work without rotating.)

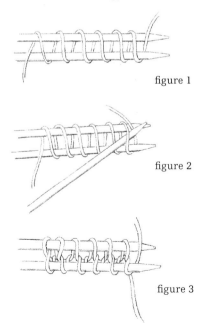

figure 1

figure 2

figure 3

LONG-TAIL (CONTINENTAL) CAST-ON

Leaving a long tail (about ½" [1.3 cm] for each stitch to be cast on), make a slipknot and place on right needle. Place thumb and index finger of your left hand between the yarn ends to that working yarn is around your index finger and tail end is around your thumb and secure the yarn ends with your other fingers. Hold your palm upward, making a V of yarn **(Figure 1)**. *Bring needle up through loop on thumb **(Figure 2)**, catch first strand around index finger, and go back down through loop on thumb **(Figure 3)**. Drop loop off thumb and, placing thumb back in V configuration, tighten resulting stitch on needle **(Figure 4)**. Repeat from * for the desired number of stitches.

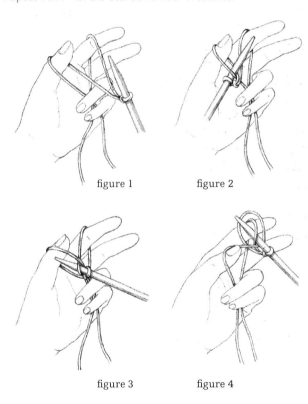

figure 1

figure 2

figure 3

figure 4

PROVISIONAL (INVISIBLE) CAST-ON

Make a loose slipknot of working yarn and place it on the right needle. Hold a length of waste yarn next to the slipknot and around your left thumb; hold working yarn over your left index finger. *Bring right needle forward under waste yarn, over working yarn, grab a loop of working yarn **(Figure 1)**, then bring needle to the front over both yarns and grab a second loop **(Figure 2)**. Repeat from * for the desired number of stitches. When you're ready to work in the opposite direction, place the exposed loops on a knitting needle as you pull out the waste yarn.

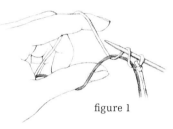

figure 1

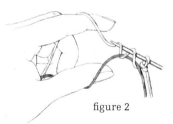

figure 2

Decreases

KNIT TWO TOGETHER (K2TOG)

Knit two stitches together as if they were a single stitch.

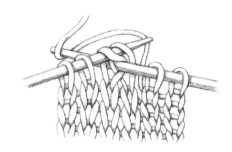

PURL TWO TOGETHER (P2TOG)

Purl two stitches together as if they were a single stitch.

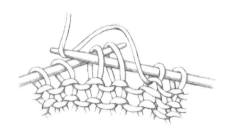

SLIP, SLIP, KNIT (SSK)

Slip two stitches individually knitwise **(Figure 1)**, insert left needle tip into the front of these two slipped stitches, and use the right needle to knit them together through their back loops **(Figure 2)**.

SLIP, SLIP, PURL (SSP)

Holding yarn in front, slip two stitches individually knitwise **(Figure 1)**, then slip these two stitches back onto left needle (they will be turned on the needle) and purl them together through their back loops **(Figure 2)**.

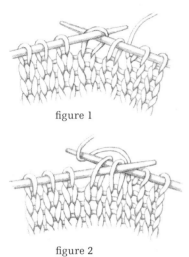

figure 1

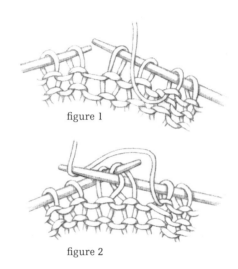

figure 1

figure 2

figure 2

SLIP, SLIP, SLIP, KNIT (SSSK)

Slip three stitches individually knitwise, insert left needle tip into the front of these three slipped stitches, and use the right needle to knit them together through their back loops.

SLIP, SLIP, SLIP, PURL (SSSP)

Holding yarn in front, slip three stitches individually knitwise, then slip these three stitches back onto left needle (they will be turned on the needle) and purl them together through their back loops.

Grafting

KITCHENER STITCH

Arrange stitches on two needles so that there is the same number of stitches on each needle. Hold the needles parallel to each other with right sides of the knitting facing up. Allowing about ½" (1.3 cm) per stitch to be grafted, thread matching yarn on a tapestry needle. Work from right to left as follows:

Step 1. Bring tapestry needle through the first stitch on the front needle as if to purl and leave the stitch on the needle **(Figure 1)**.

Step 2. Bring tapestry needle through the first stitch on the back needle as if to knit and leave that stitch on the needle **(Figure 2)**.

Step 3. Bring tapestry needle through the first front stitch as if to knit and slip this stitch off the needle, then bring seaming needle through the next front stitch as if to purl and leave this stitch on the needle **(Figure 3)**.

Step 4. Bring tapestry needle through the first back stitch as if to purl and slip this stitch off the needle, then bring tapestry needle through the next back stitch as if to knit and leave this stitch on the needle **(Figure 4)**.

Repeat Steps 3 and 4 until no stitches remain on the needles, adjusting the tension to match the rest of the knitting as you go.

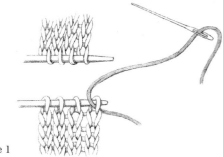

figure 1

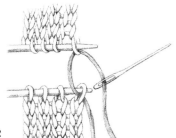

figure 2

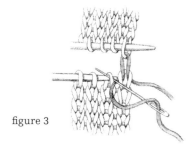

figure 3

figure 4

Increases

KNIT ONE FRONT AND BACK (K1F&B)

Knit into a stitch but leave it on the left needle **(Figure 1)**, then knit through the back loop of the same stitch **(Figure 2)** and slip the original stitch off the needle.

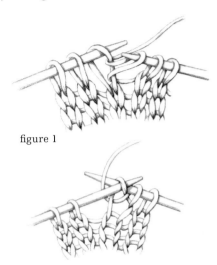

figure 1

figure 2

MAKE ONE (M1L)

With left needle tip, lift the strand between last knitted stitch and first stitch on left needle from front to back **(Figure 1)**, then knit the lifted loop through the back **(Figure 2)**. Note: when a direction is given, use this increase for M1.

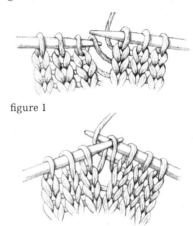

figure 1

figure 2

MAKE ONE RIGHT (M1R)

With left needle tip, lift the strand between the needles from back to front **(Figure 1)**. Knit the lifted loop through the front **(Figure 2)**.

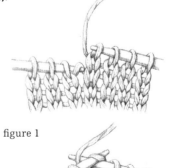

figure 1

figure 2

MAKE ONE PURLWISE RIGHT (M1PR)

With left needle tip, lift strand between needles from back to front **(Figure 1)**. Purl lifted loop **(Figure 2)**.

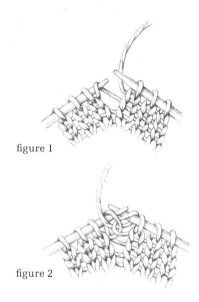

figure 1

figure 2

MAKE ONE PURLWISE LEFT (M1PL)

With left needle tip, lift the strand between the needles from front to back, then purl the lifted loop through the back.

YO (YARNOVER)

Wrap the working yarn around the needle from front to back, then bring yarn into position to work the next stitch (leave it in back if a knit stitch follows; bring it under the needle to the front if a purl stitch follows) **(Figure 1)**. To work a double yarnover, wrap the working yarn and the needle twice **(Figure 2)**.

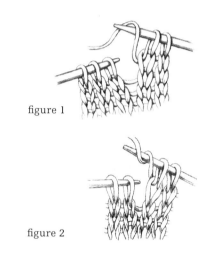

figure 1

figure 2

Pick Up and Knit

With right side facing and working from right to left, pick up stitches by inserting tip of left needle into the back half of each stitch along the selvedge edge. Knit the picked-up stitch through the back loop to twist it for a tighter join.

Short-Rows

SHORT-ROWS (KNIT SIDE)

Work to turning point, slip next stitch purlwise to right needle, then bring the yarn to the front **(Figure 1)**. Slip the same stitch back to the left needle **(Figure 2)**, turn the work around and bring the yarn in position for the next stitch, wrapping the slipped stitch with working yarn as you do so. When you come to a wrapped stitch on a subsequent row, hide the wrap by working it together with the wrapped stitch as follows: Insert right needle tip under the wrap (from the front if wrapped stitch is a knit stitch; from the back if wrapped stitch is a purl stitch), then into the stitch on the needle, and work the stitch and its wrap together as a single stitch.

SHORT-ROWS (PURL SIDE)

Work to the turning point, slip the next stitch purlwise to the right needle, bring the yarn to the back of the work **(Figure 1)**, return the slipped stitch to the left needle, bring the yarn to the front between the needles **(Figure 2)**, and turn the work so that the knit side is facing—one stitch has been wrapped and the yarn is correctly positioned to knit the next stitch. To hide the wrap on a subsequent purl row, work to the wrapped stitch, use the tip of the right needle to pick up the wrap from the back, place it on the left needle **(Figure 3)**, then purl it together with the wrapped stitch.

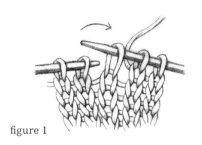

figure 1

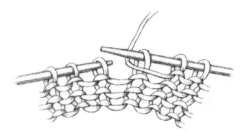

figure 1

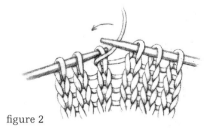

figure 2

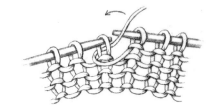

figure 2

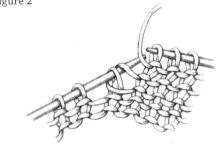

figure 3

Artyarns
39 Westmoreland Ave.
White Plains, NY 10606
artyarns.com
Ultramerino 4

Blue Moon Fiber Arts Inc.
56587 Mollenhour Rd.
Scappoose, OR 97056
Socks That Rock Lightweight

Claudia Hand Painted Yarns
40 W. Washington St.
Harrisonburg, VA 22802
claudiaco.com
Fingering

Colinette Yarns
Distributed in the United States by
   Unique Kolours
28 N. Bacton Hill Rd.
Malvern, PA 19355
uniquekolours.com
Jitterbug

Cookie A Knitwear Design
cookiea.com

Dream in Color Yarns
907 Atlantic Ave.
West Chicago, IL 60185
dreamincoloryarns.com
Smooshy

Fleece Artist
fleeceartist.com
2/6 Merino

Hand Jive Knits
handjiveknits.com
Nature's Palette Fingering Weight

Koigu Wool Designs
PO Box 158
Chatsworth, ON
Canada N0H1G0
koigu.com
Koigu Premium Merino

Lana Grossa
Distributed in the United States by
   Muench Yarns
1323 Scott St.
Petaluma, CA 94954-1135
muenchyarns.com
Meilenweit 50 Seta/Cashmere

Lorna's Laces
4229 North Honore St.
Chicago, IL 60613
lornaslaces.net
Shepherd Sock

Louet North America
3425 Hands Rd.
Prescott, ON
Canada K0E1T0
louet.com
Gems Fingering Weight

Mountain Colors
PO Box 156
Corvallis, MT 59828
mountaincolors.com
Bearfoot

Opal Sock Yarn
Distributed in the United States by Tutto
   Opal-Isager
137 West Water St., Ste. 220
Santa Fe, NM 87508
opalsockyarn.com
Opal Uni-Color

Shelridge Farm
c/o Buffy Taylor
PO Box 1345
Durham, ON
Canada N0G1R0
shelridge.com
Soft Touch Ultra Fingering

ShibuiKnits LLC
1101 SW Alder St.
Portland, OR 97205
shibuiknits.com
Sock

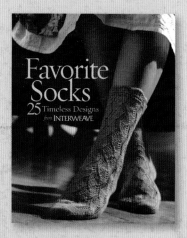

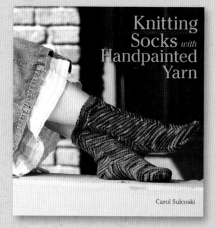